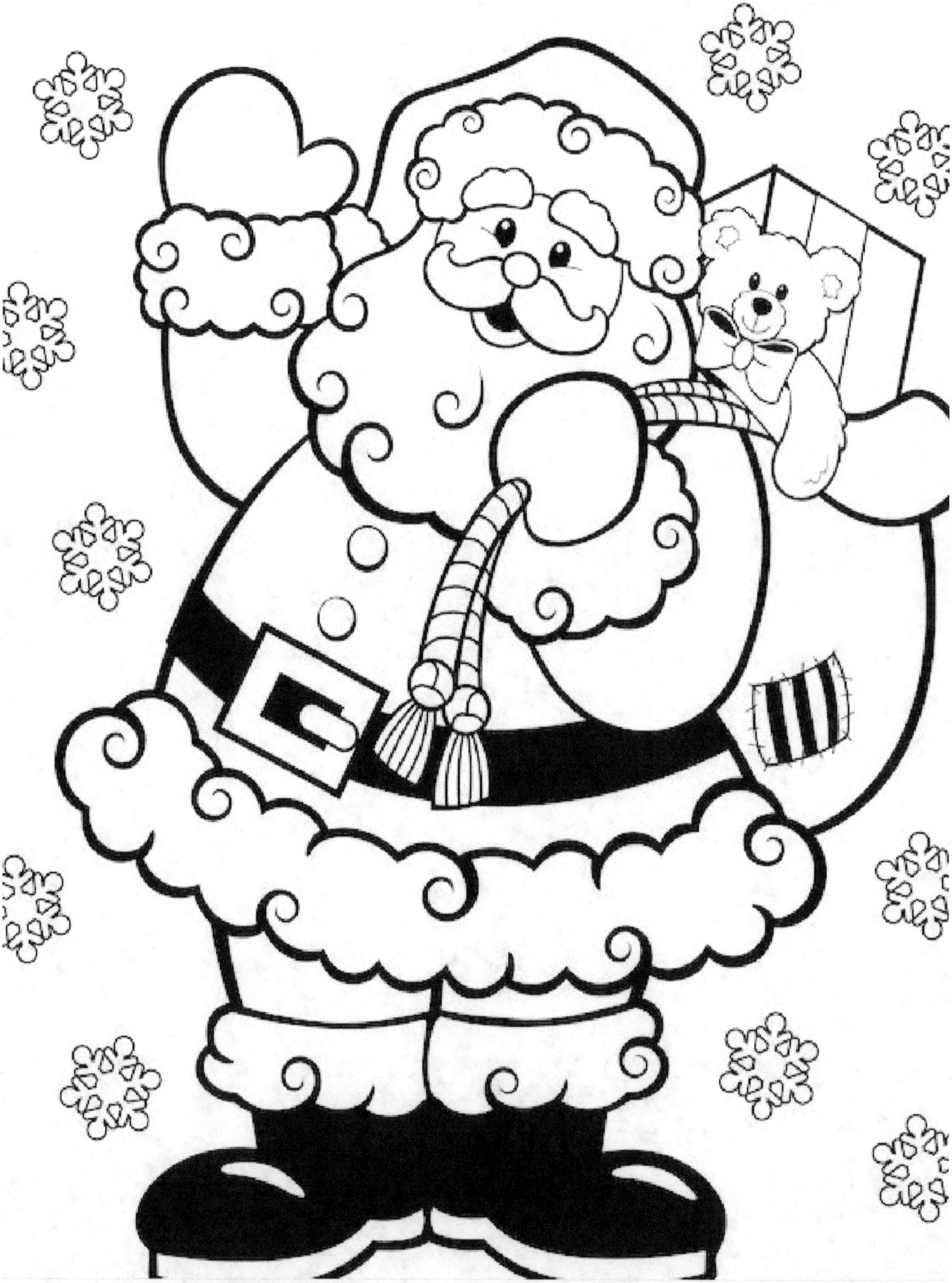

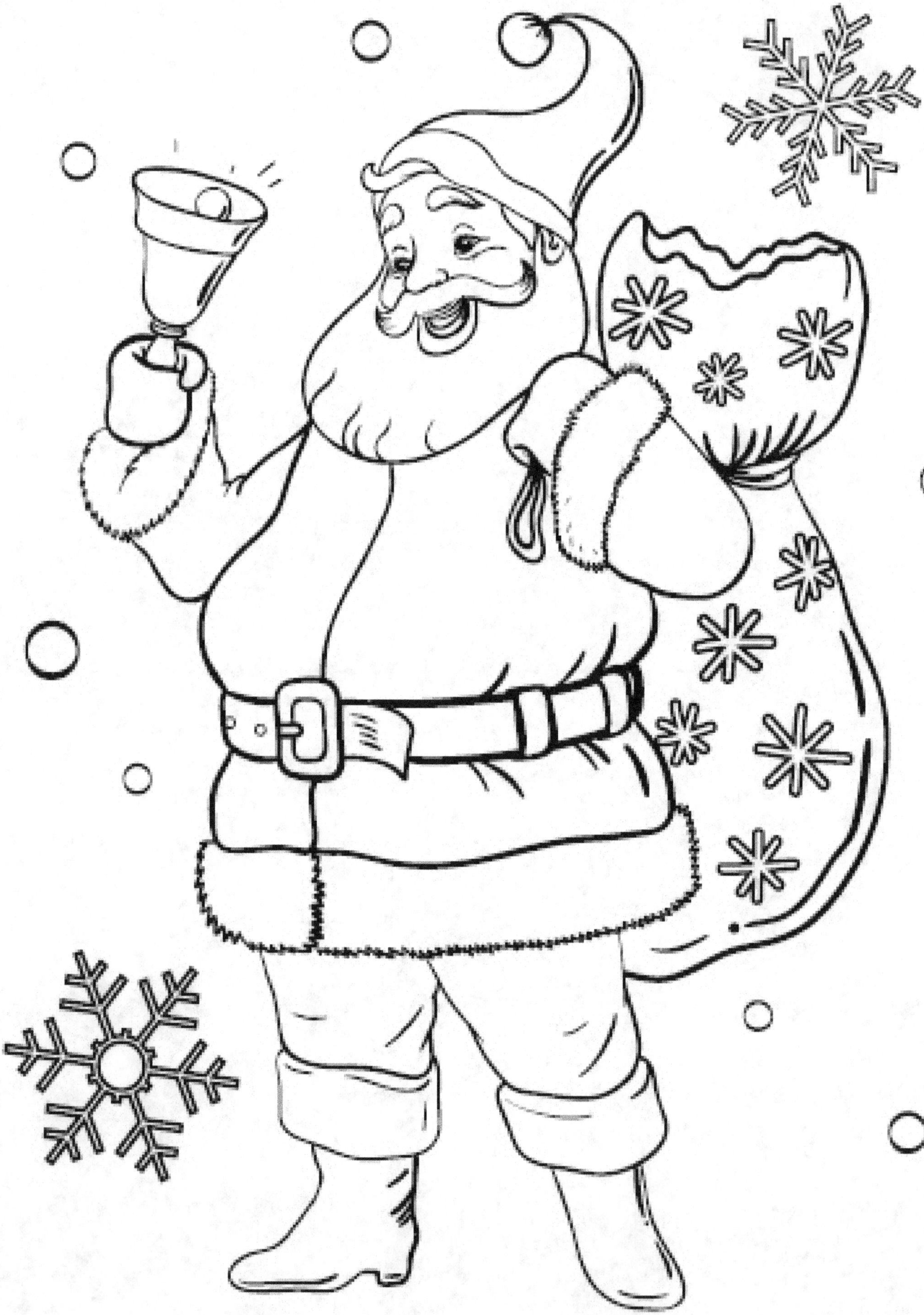

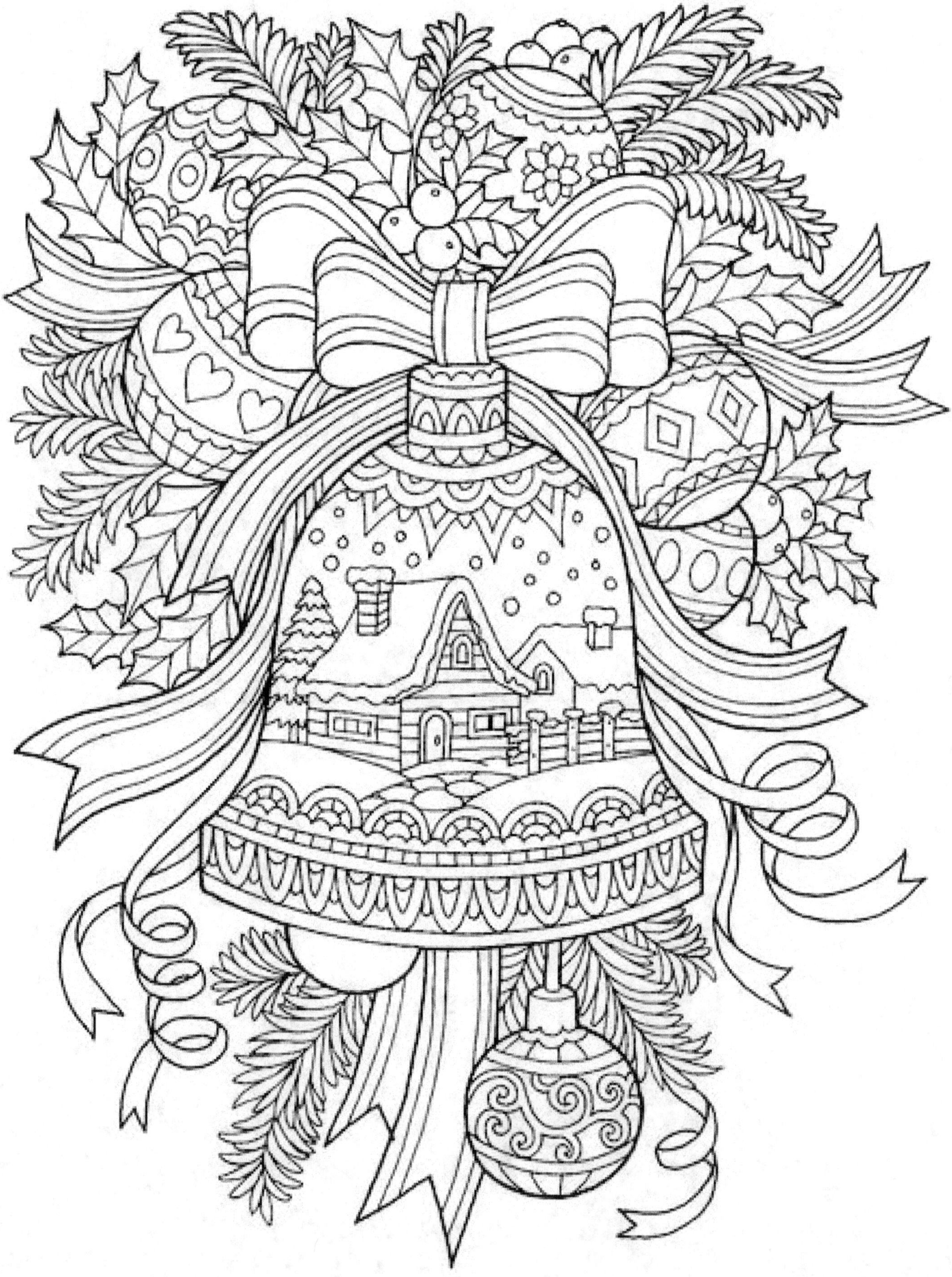

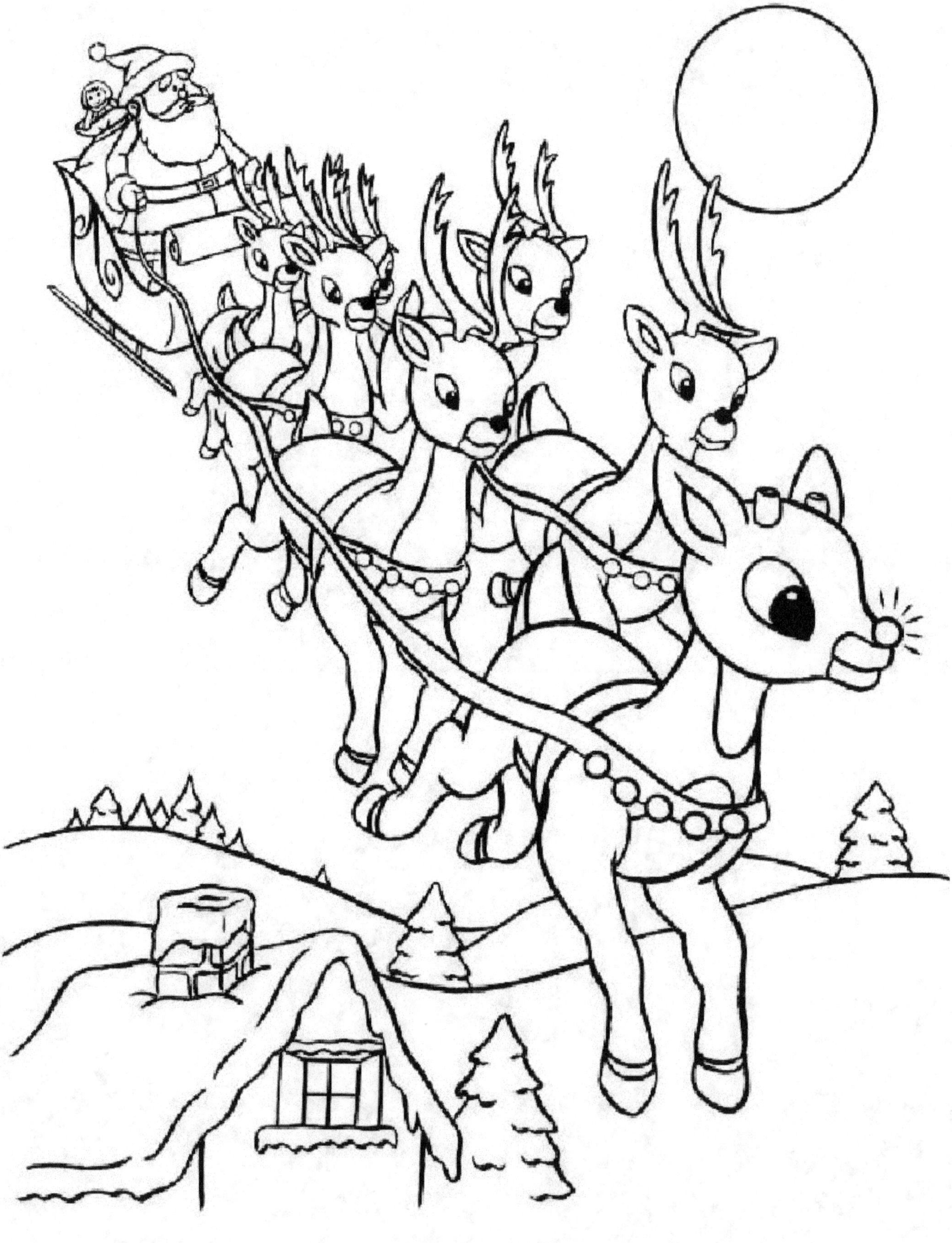

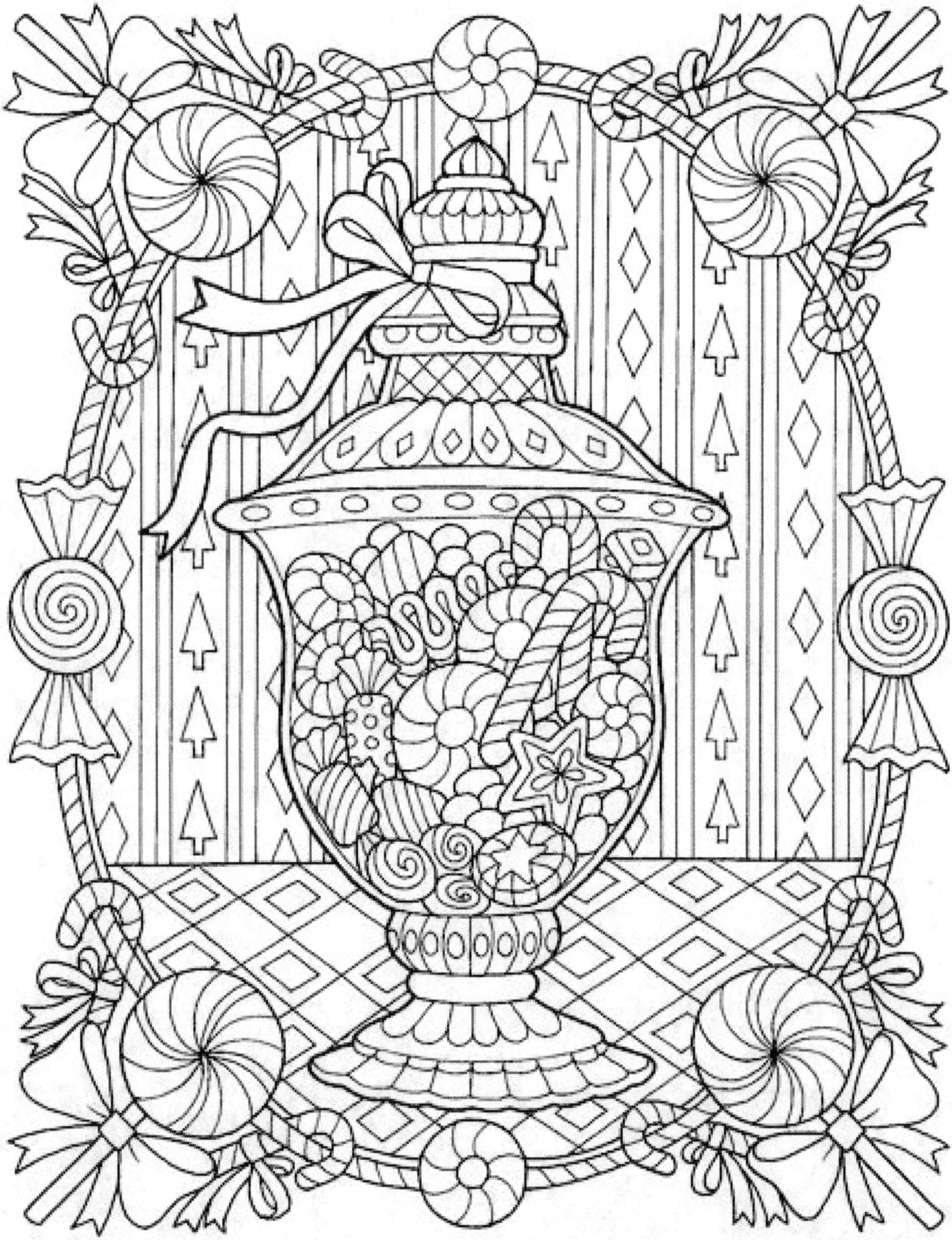

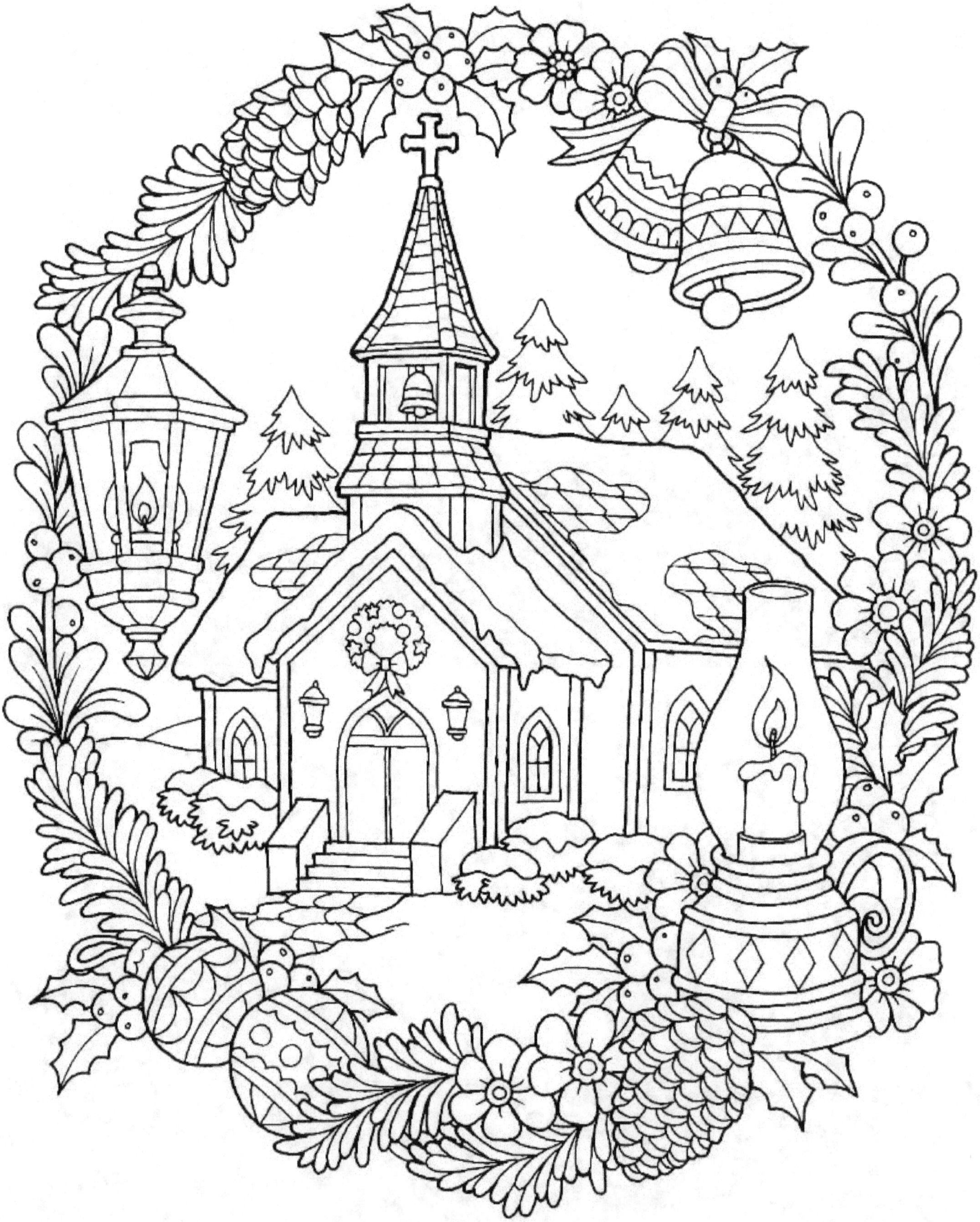

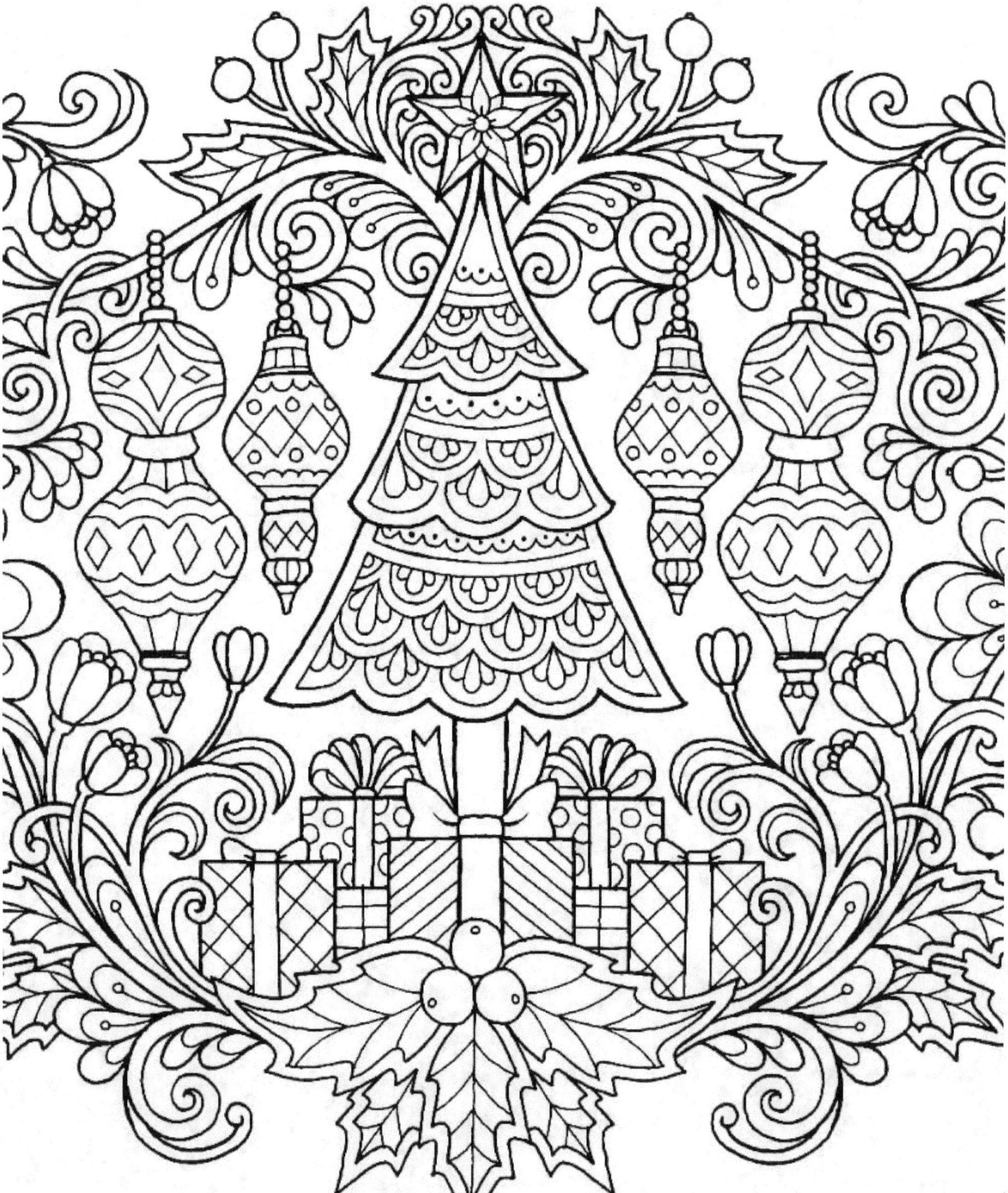

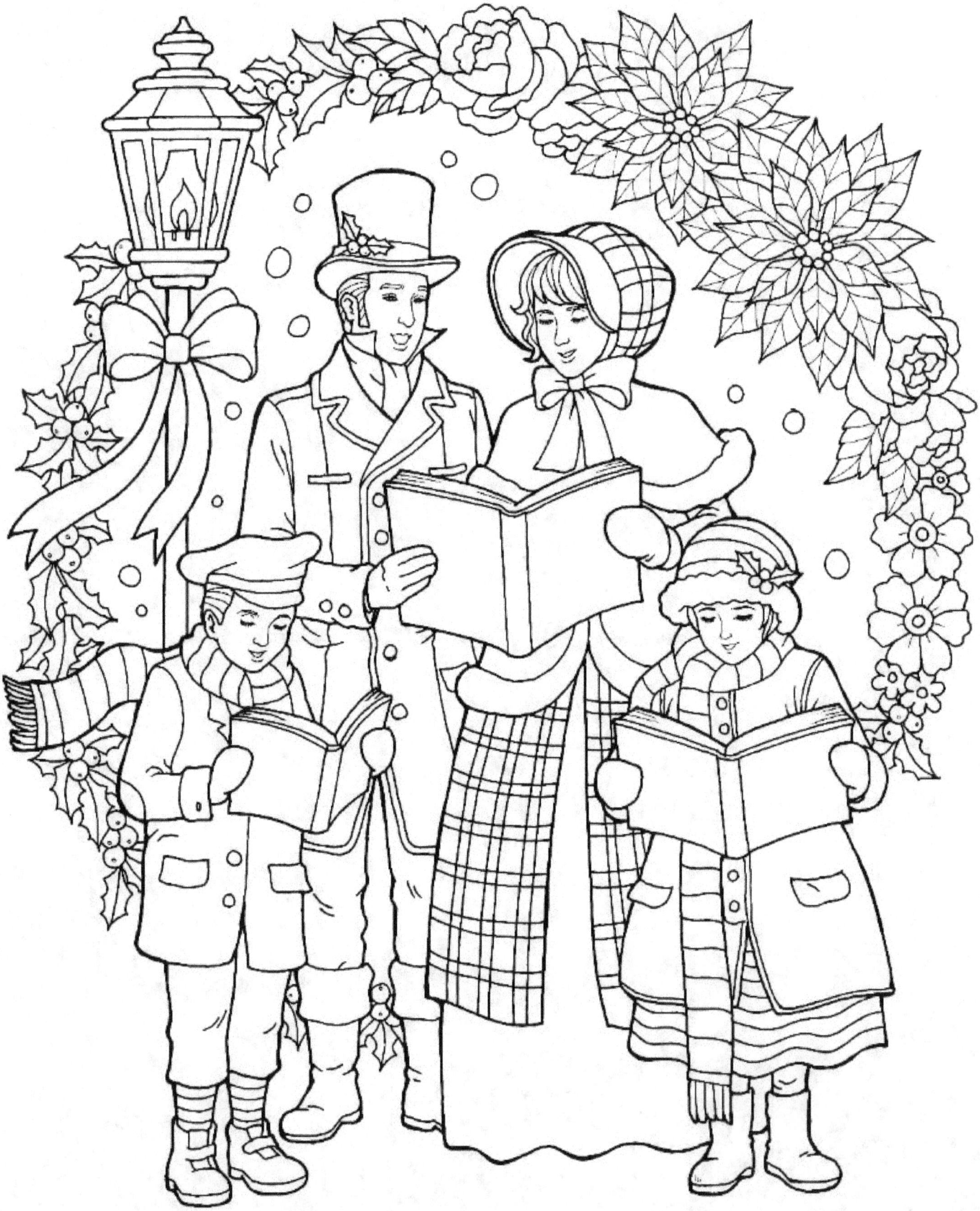

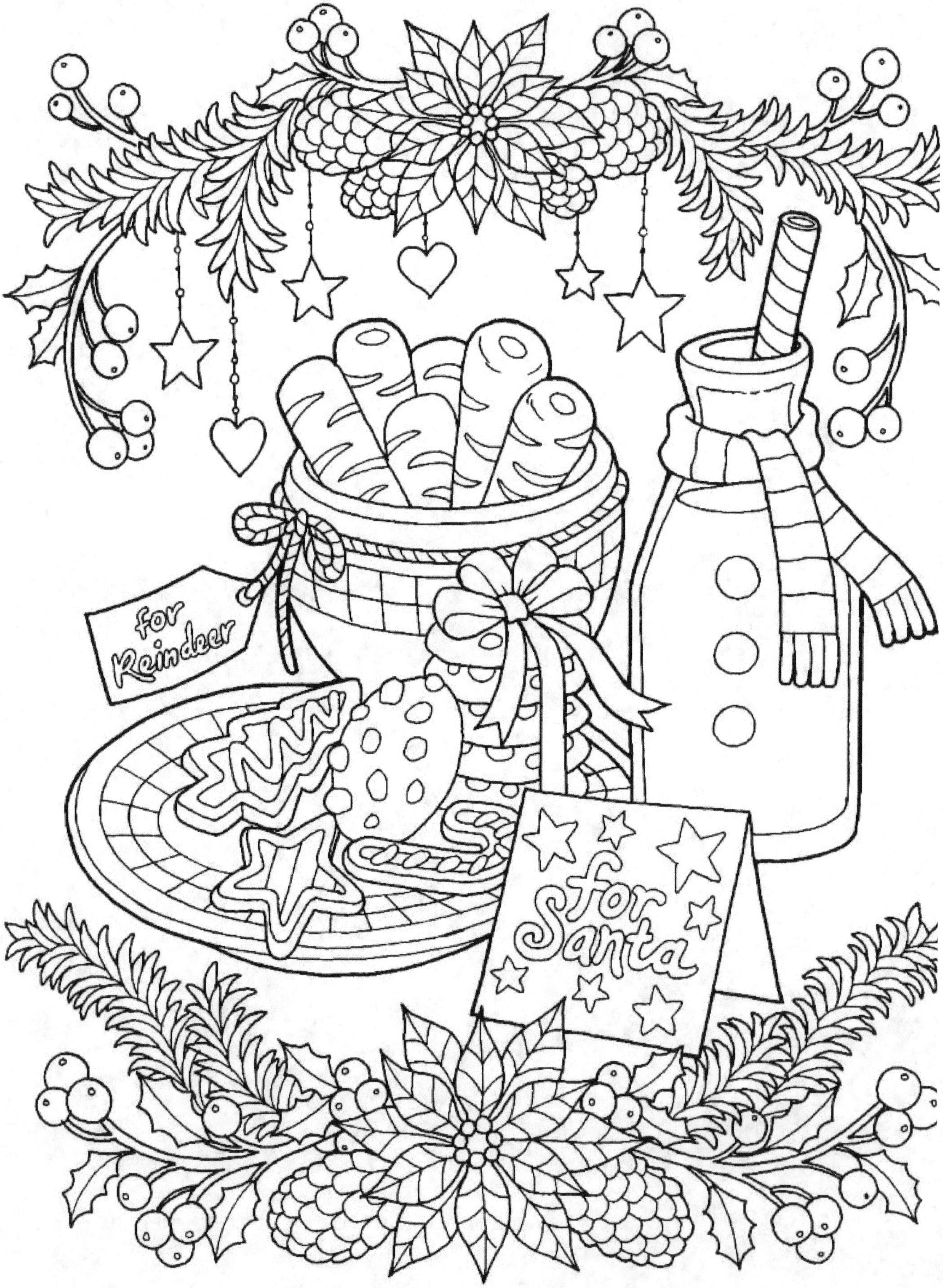
for Reindeer
for Santa

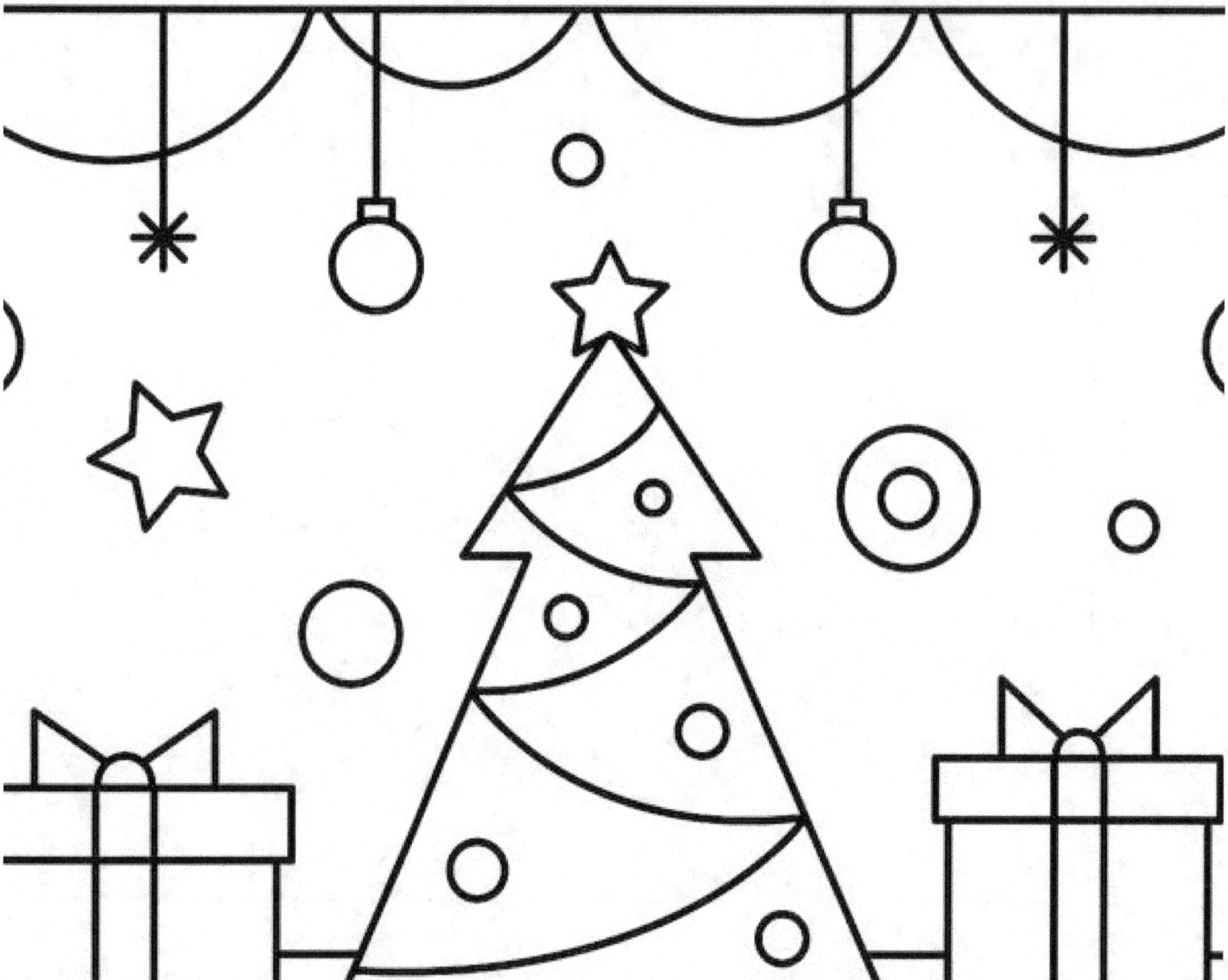
MERRY
CHRISTMAS

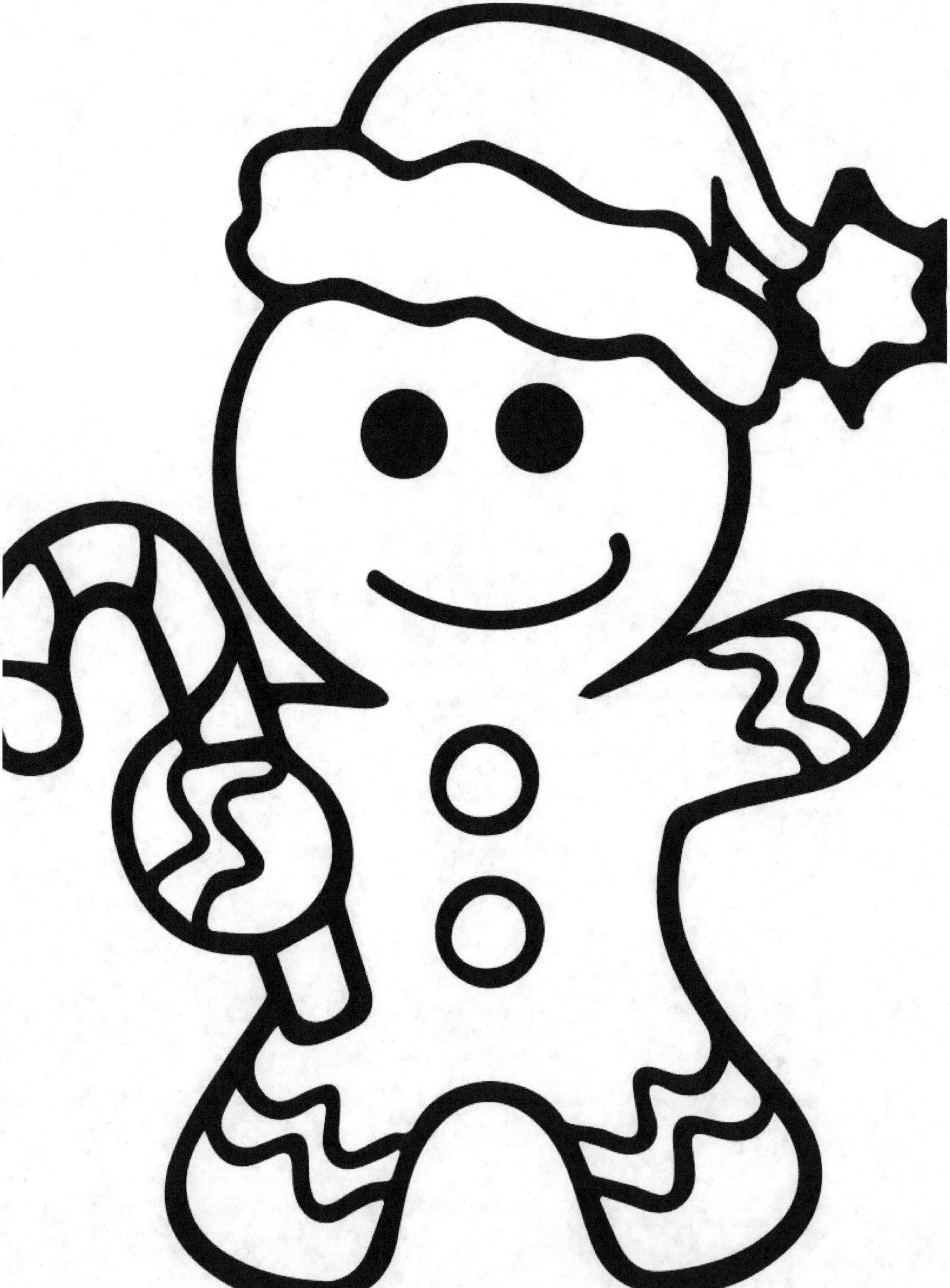

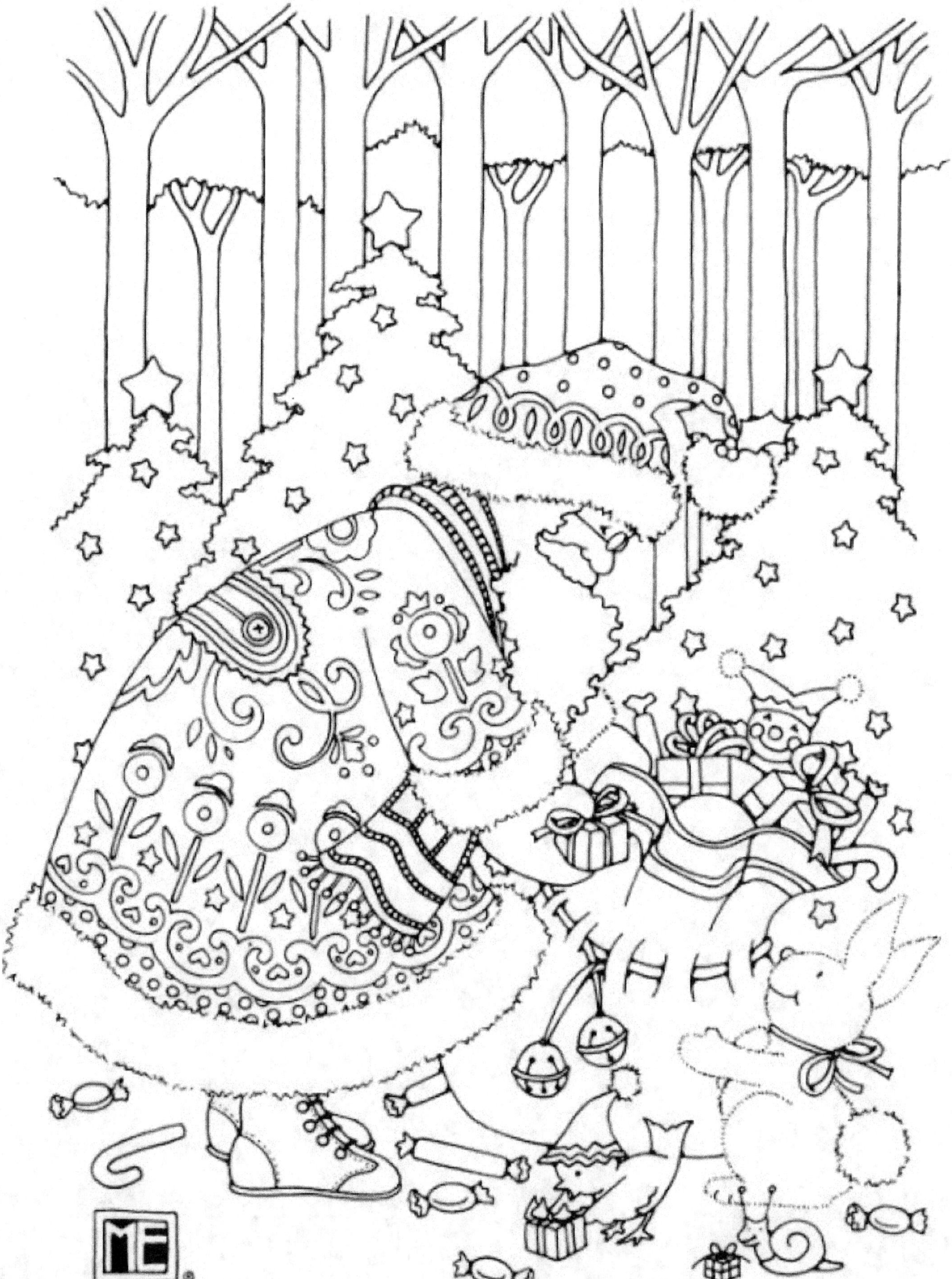

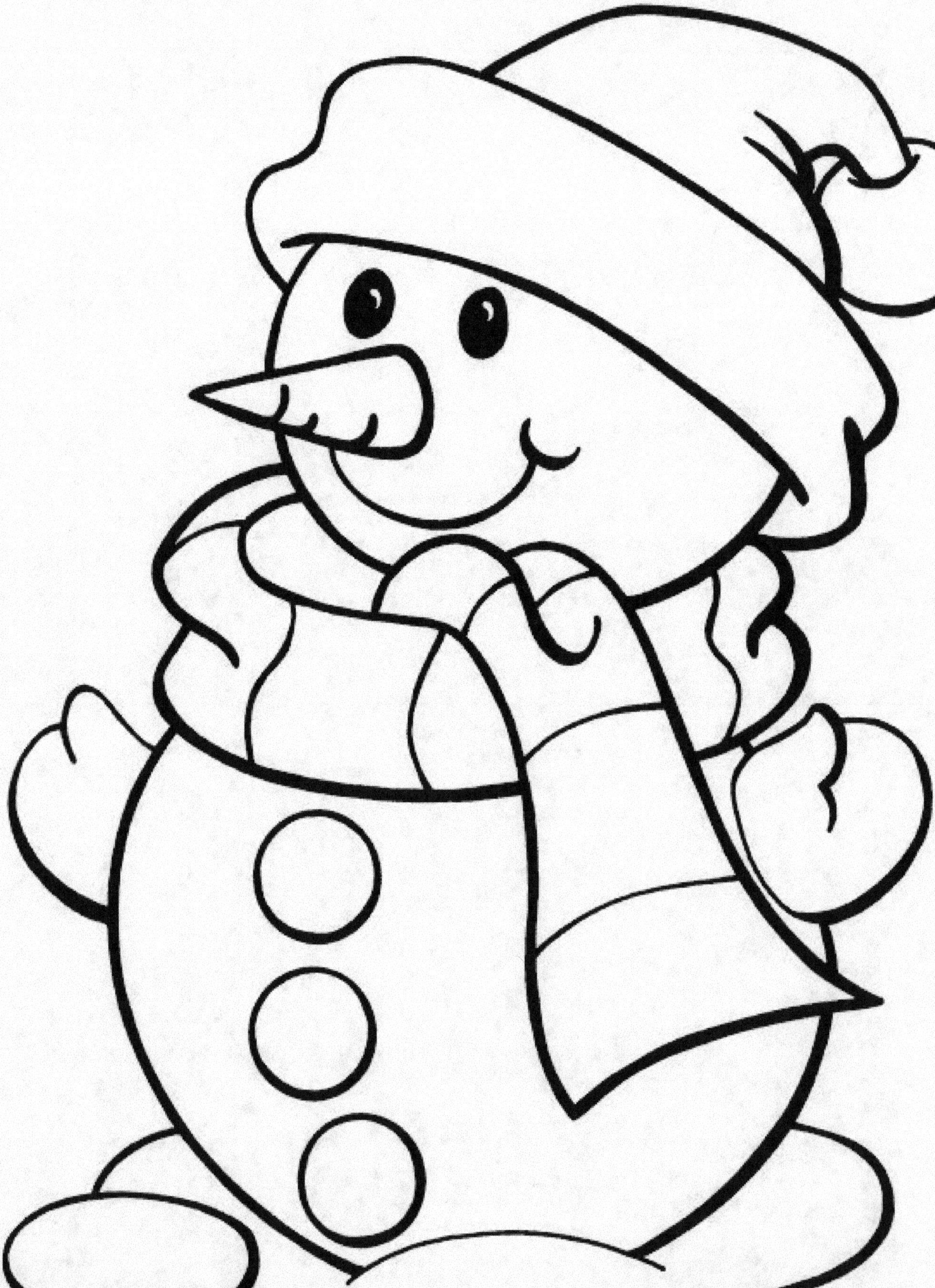

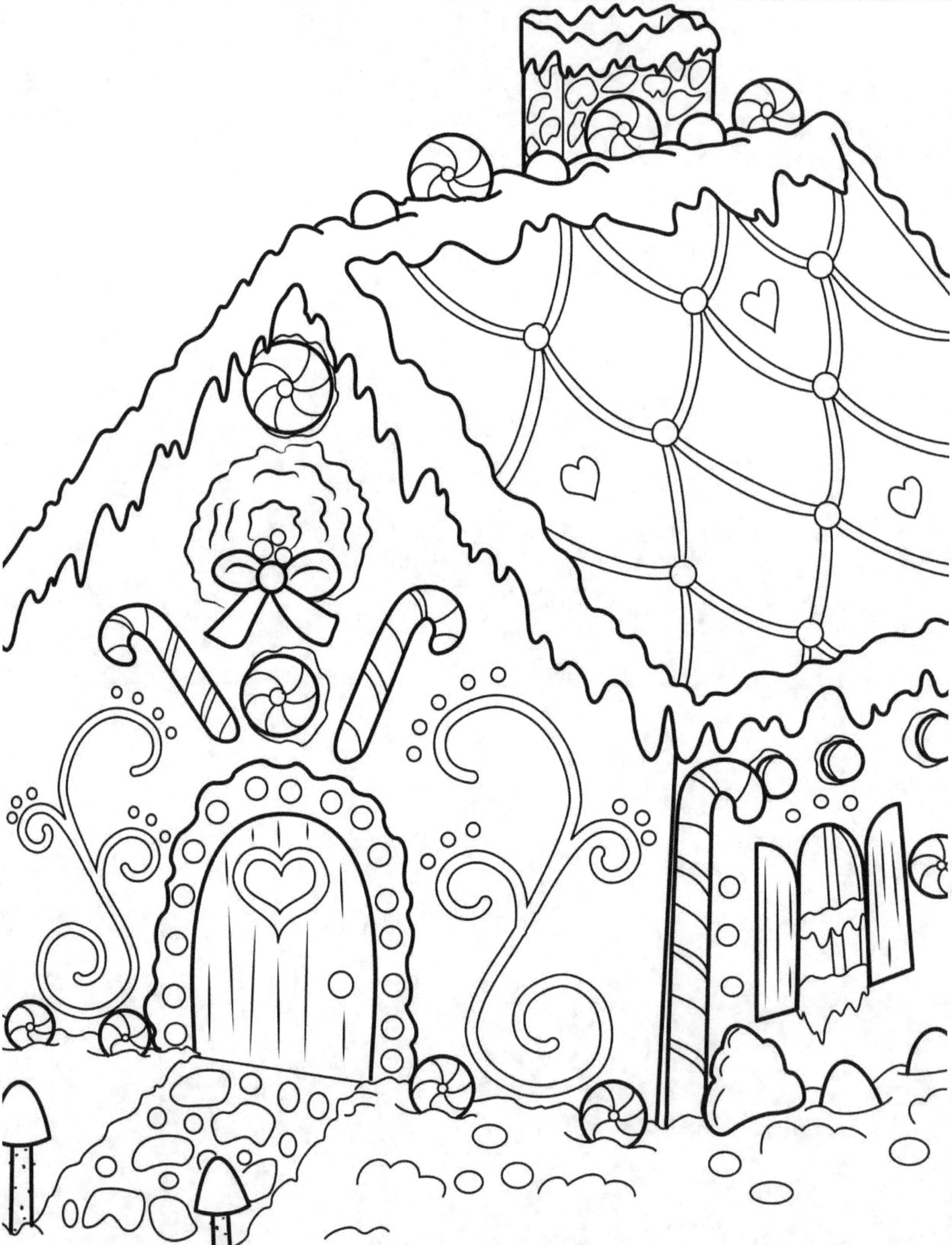

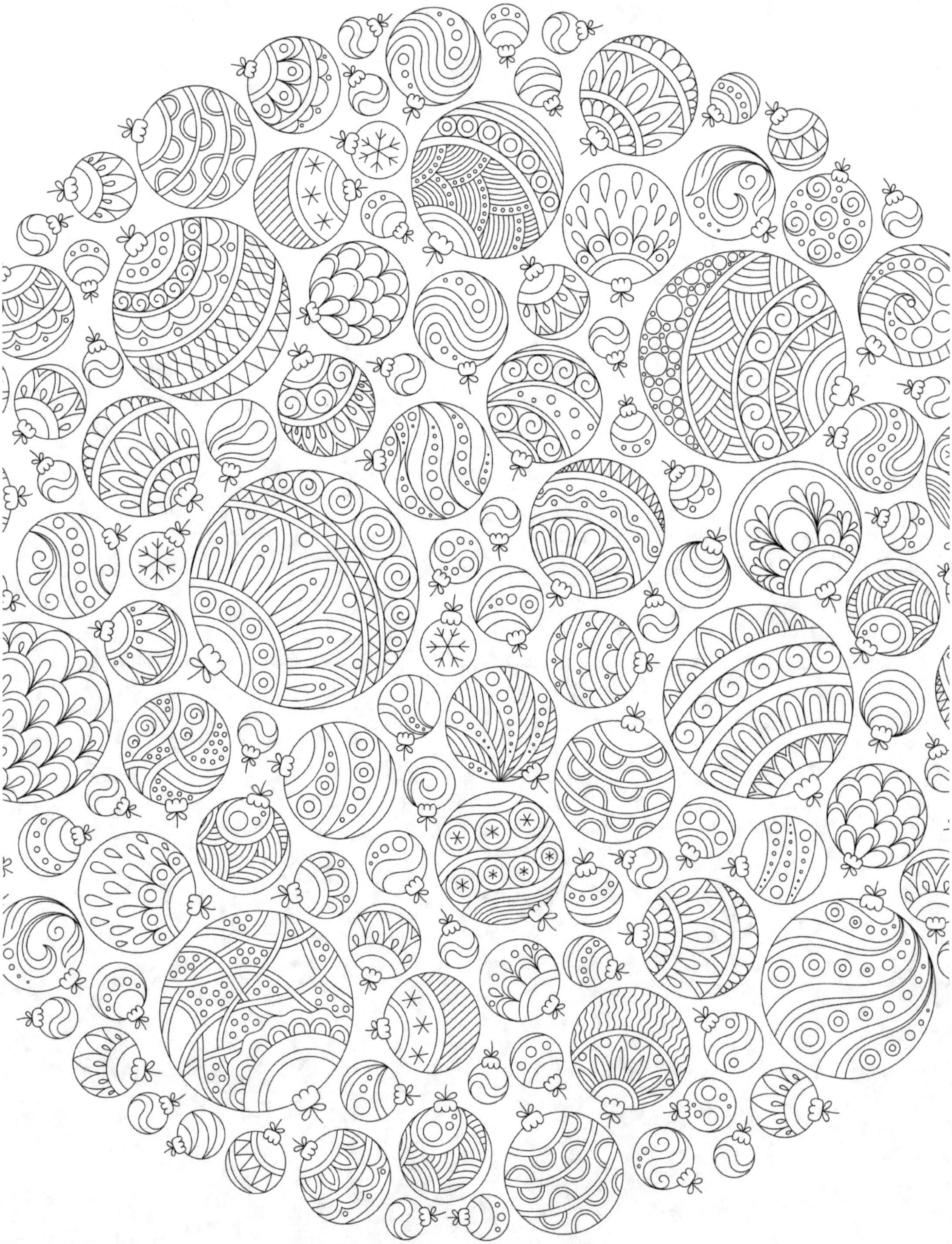

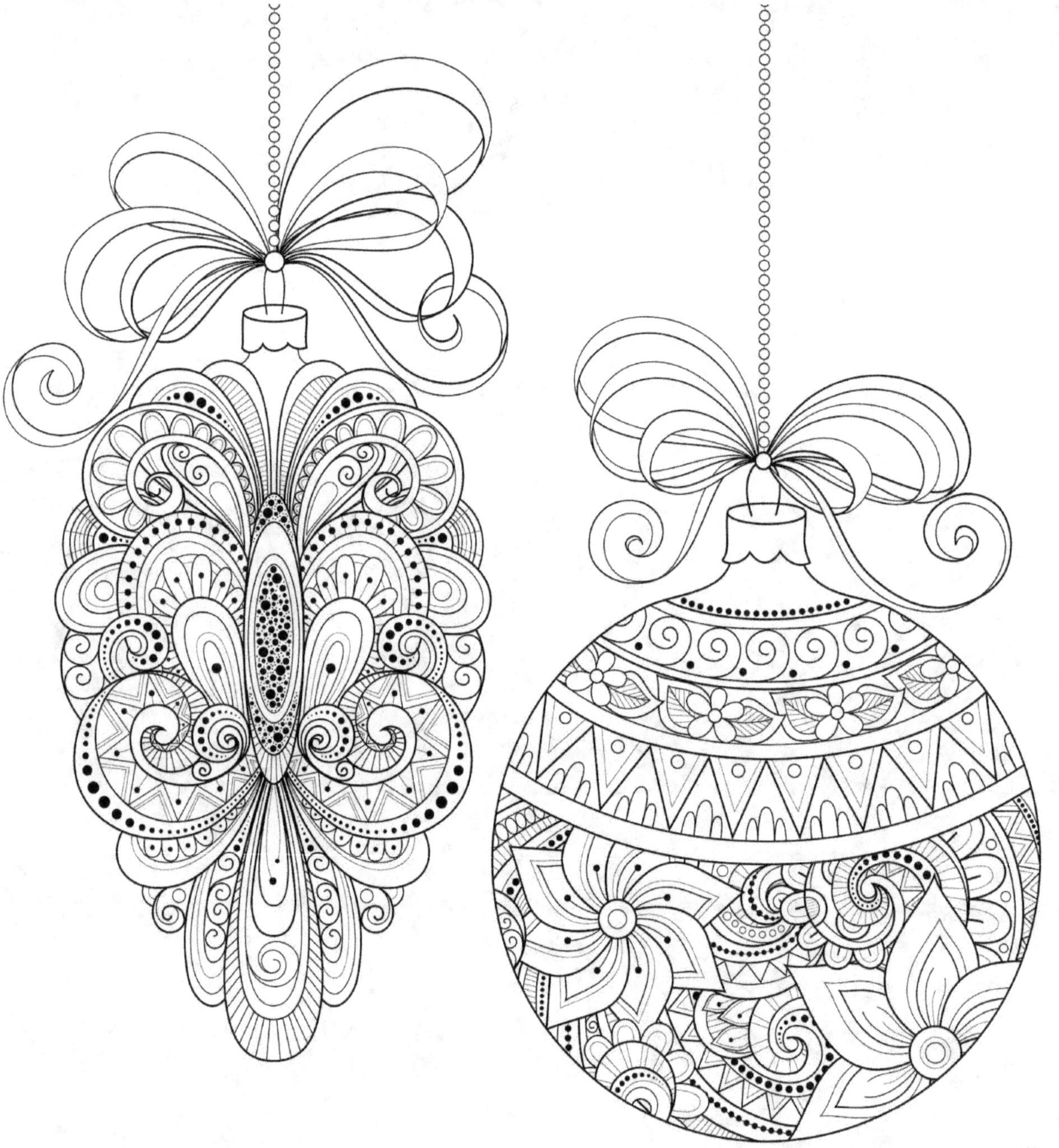

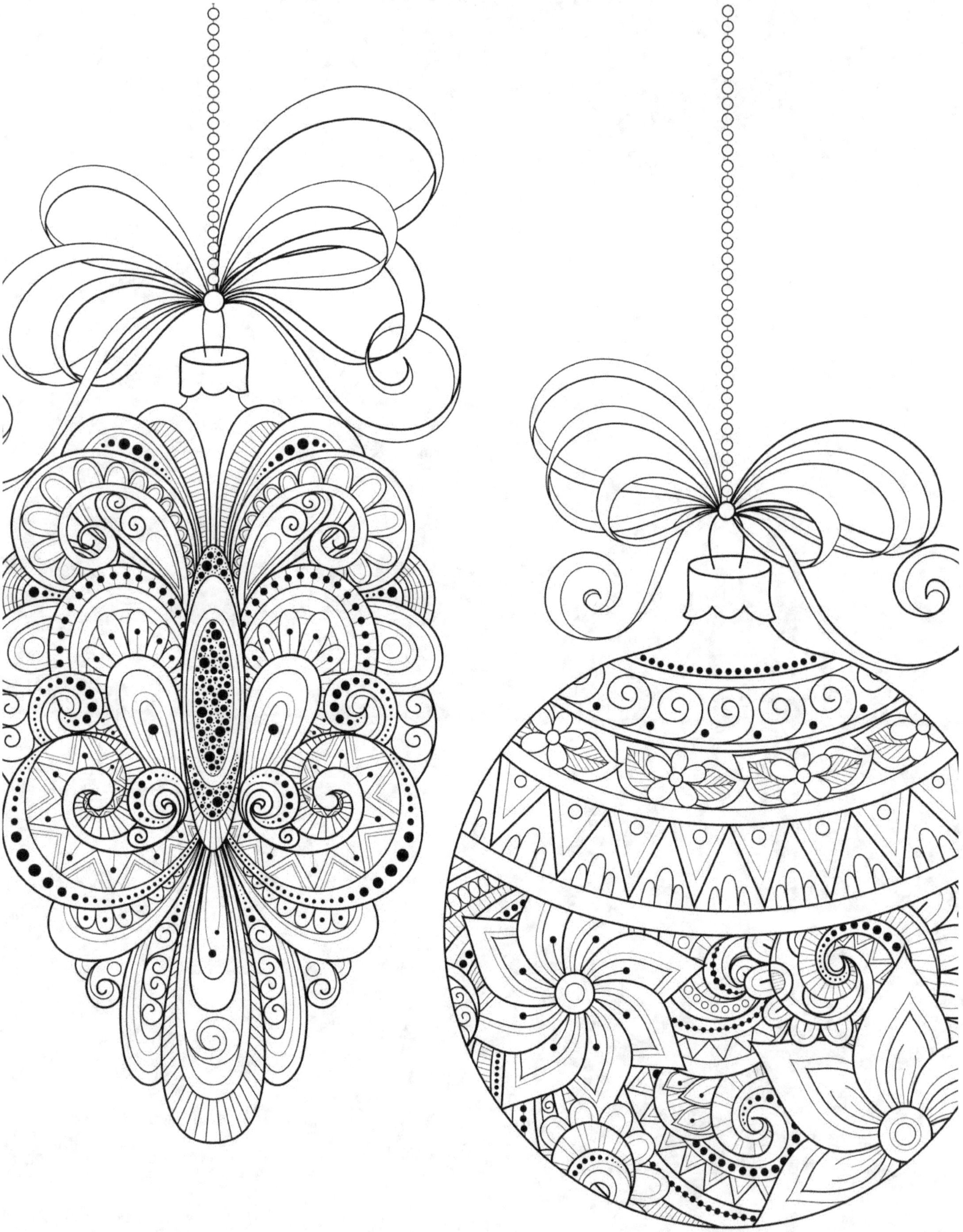

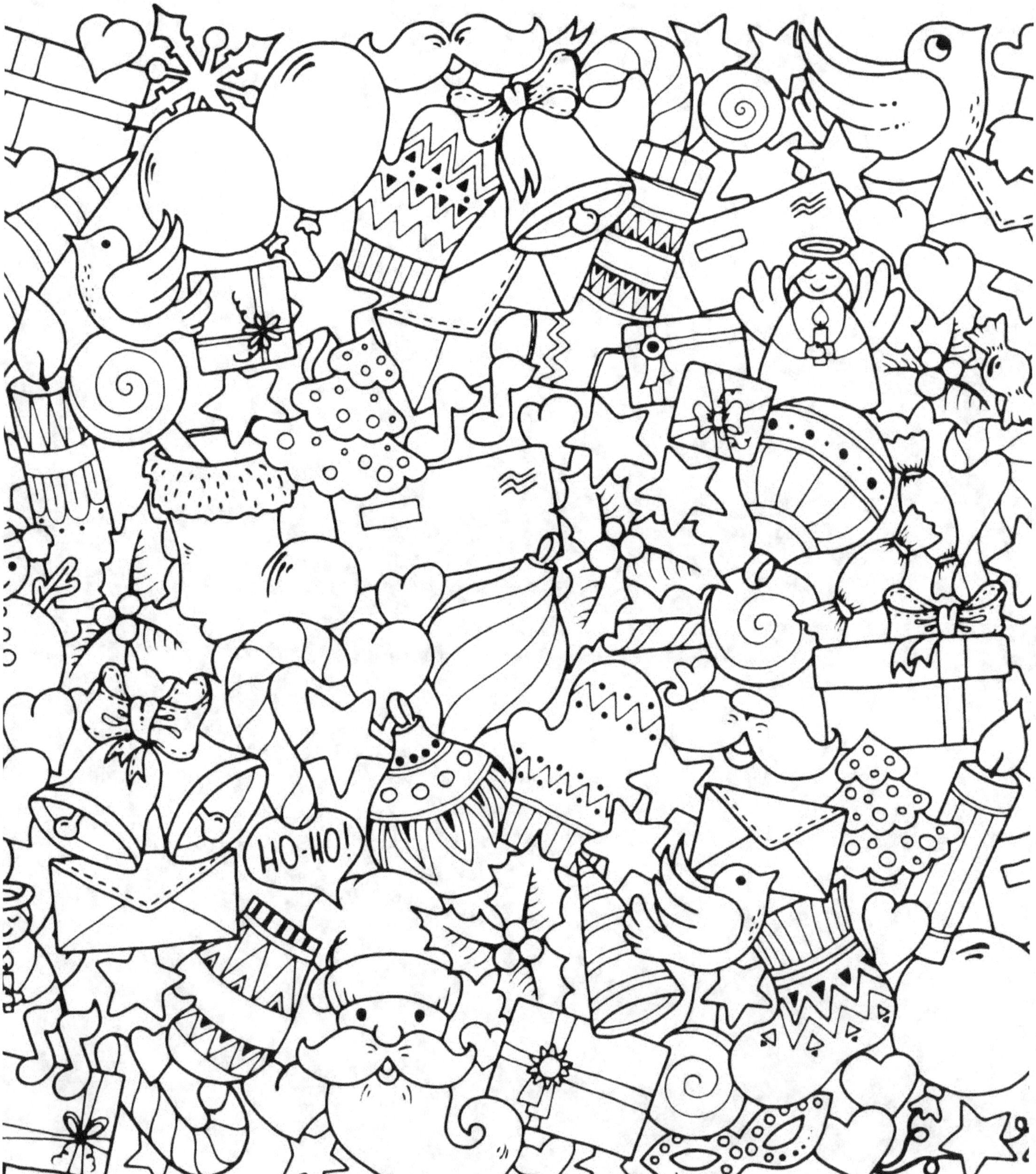
HO-HO!

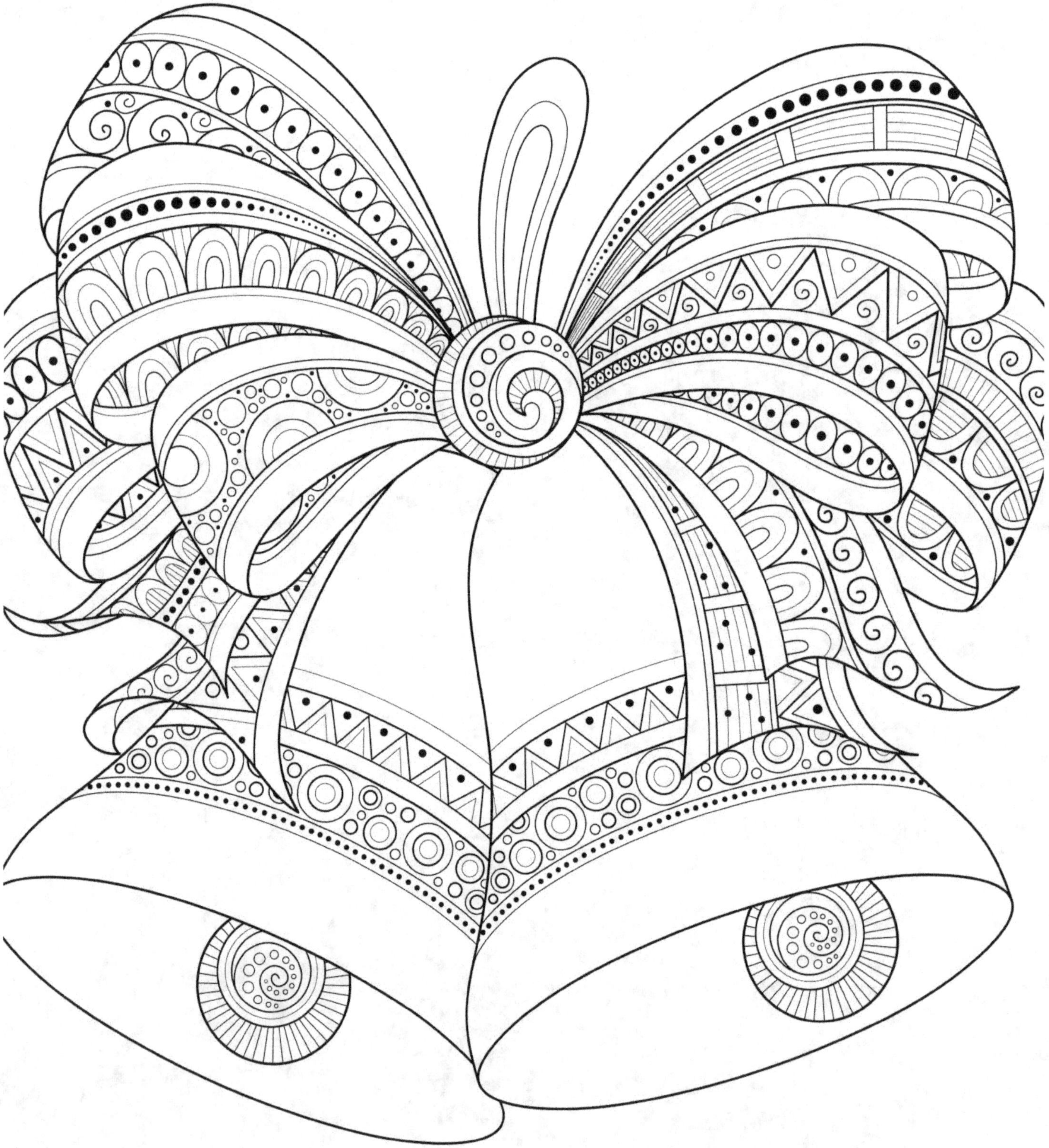

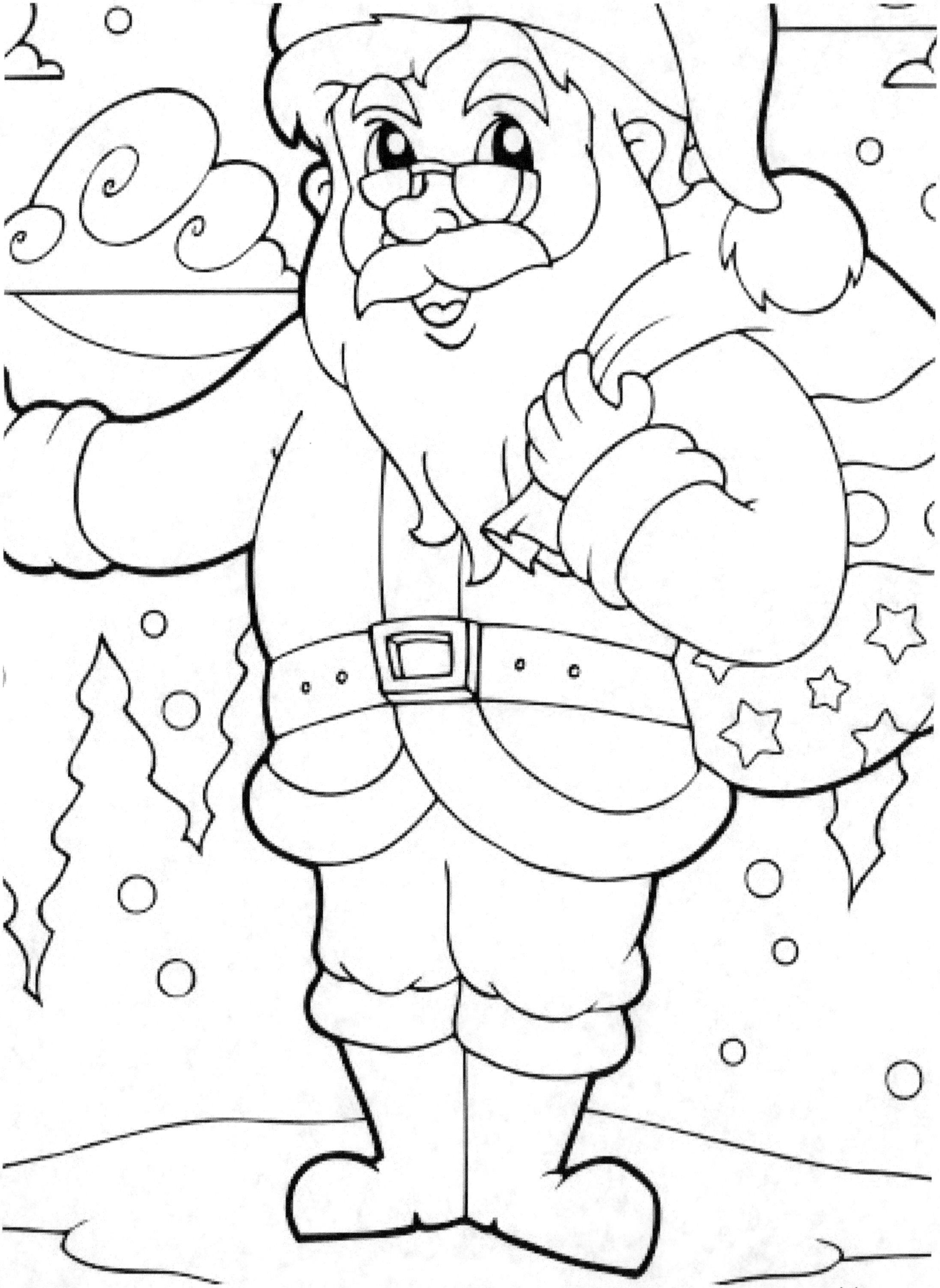

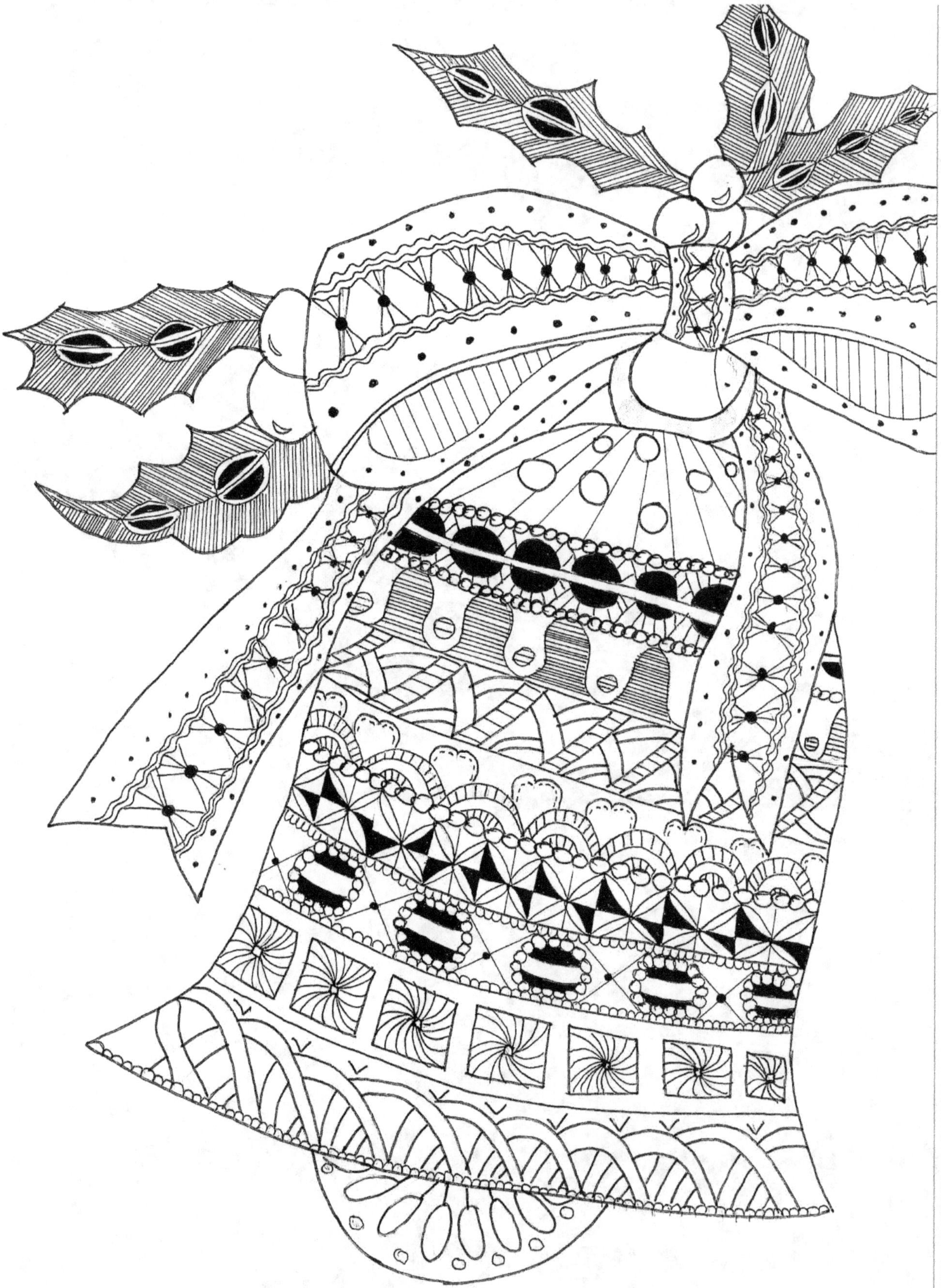

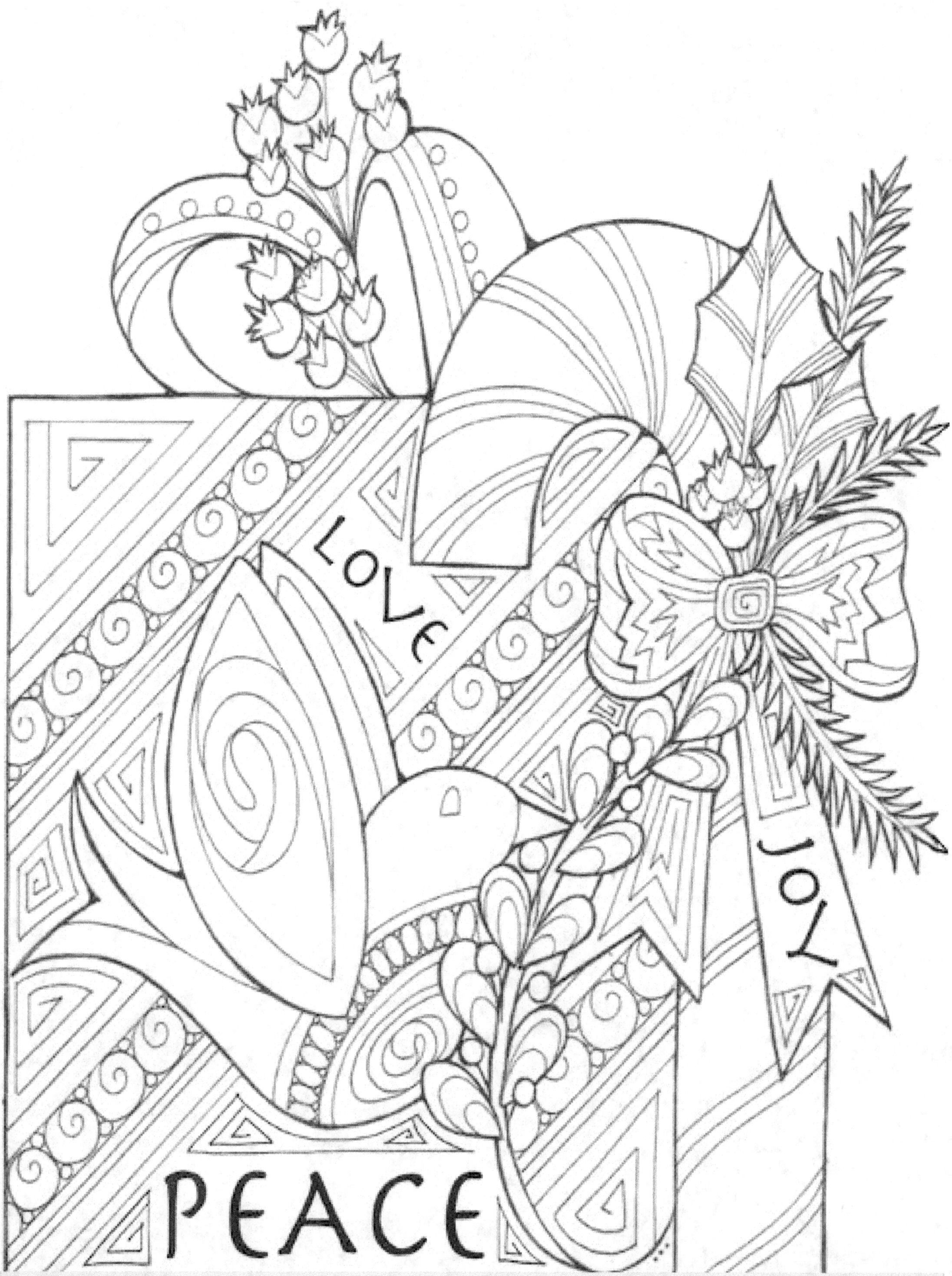
LOVE
JOY
PEACE

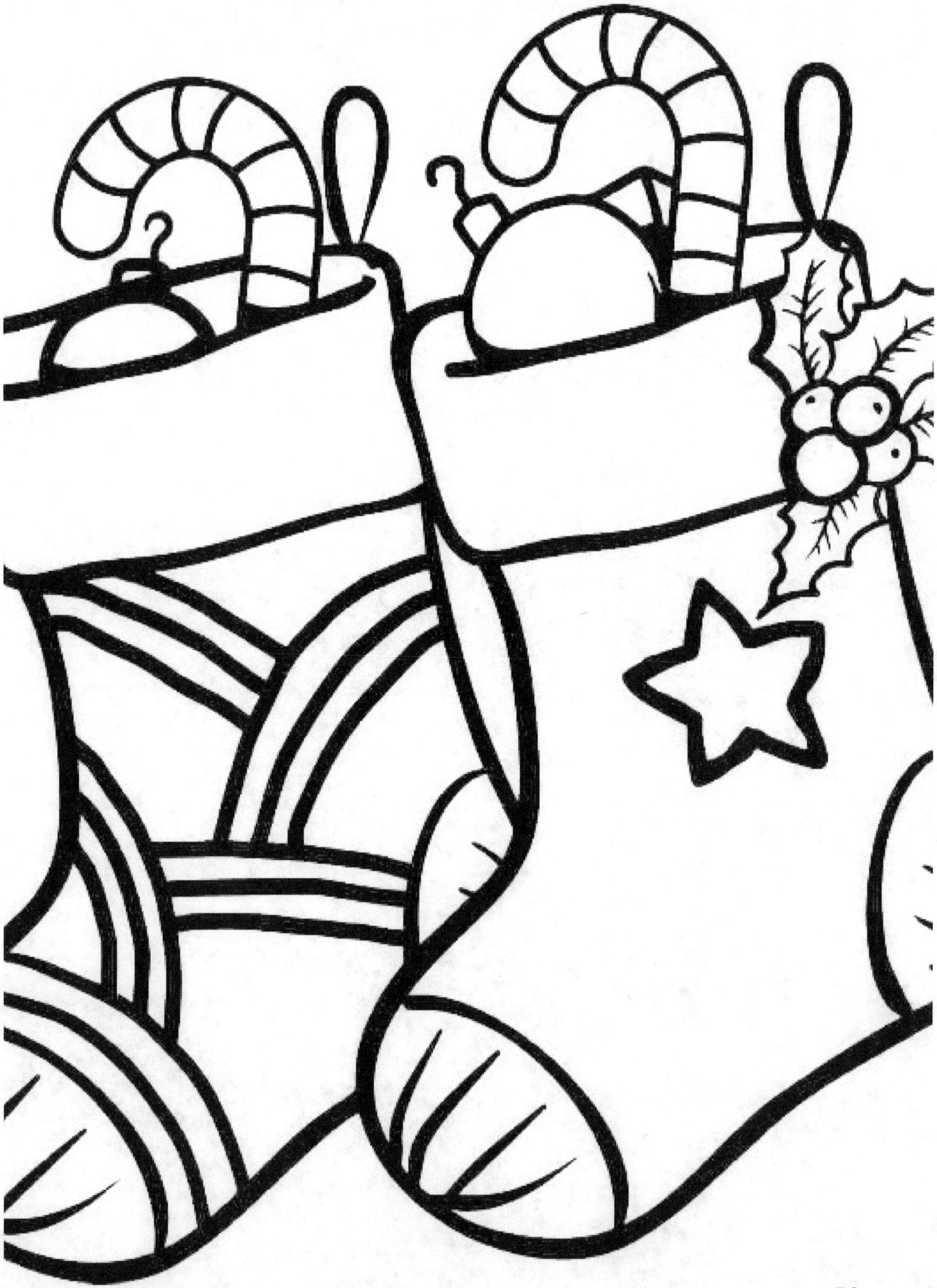

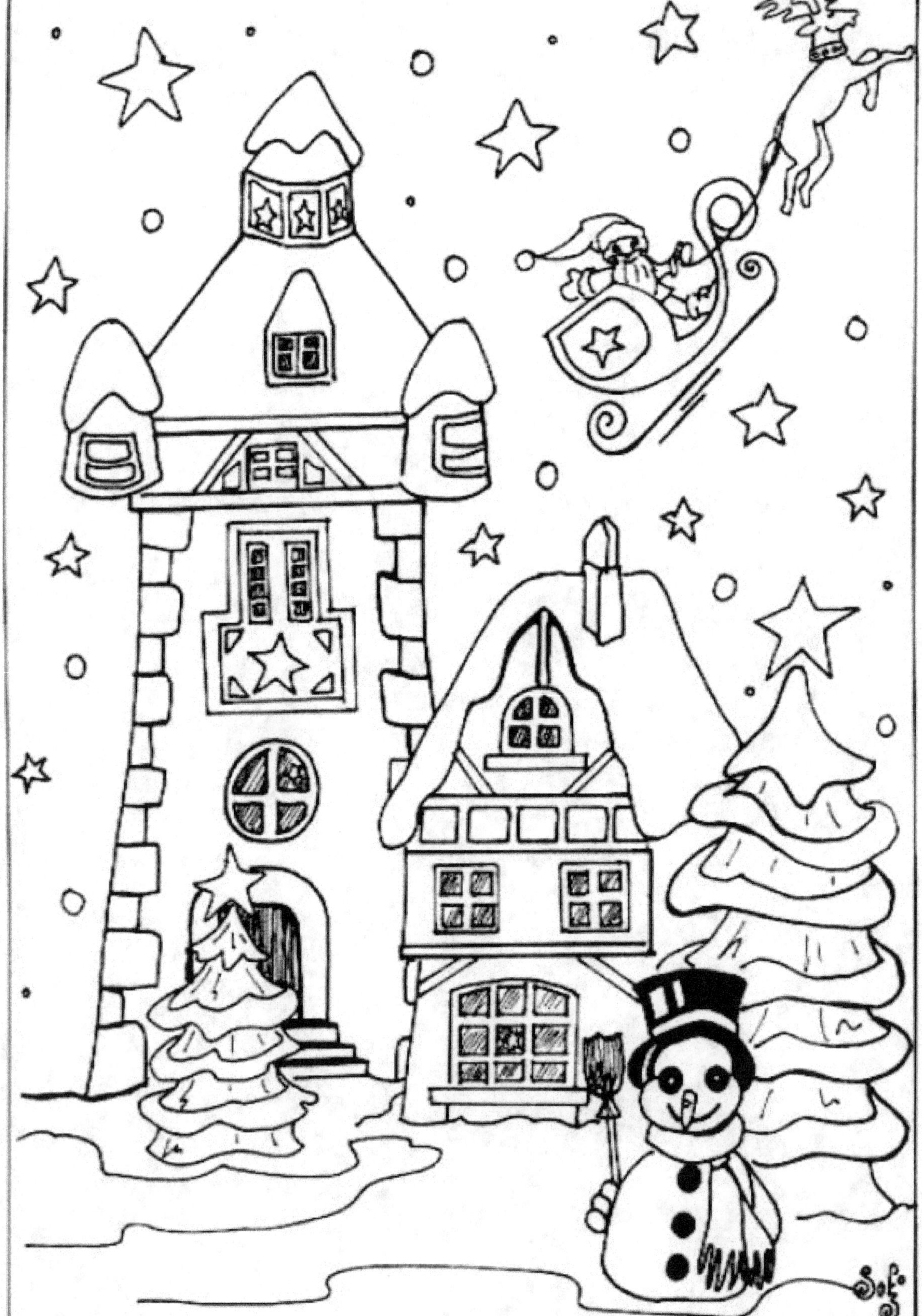

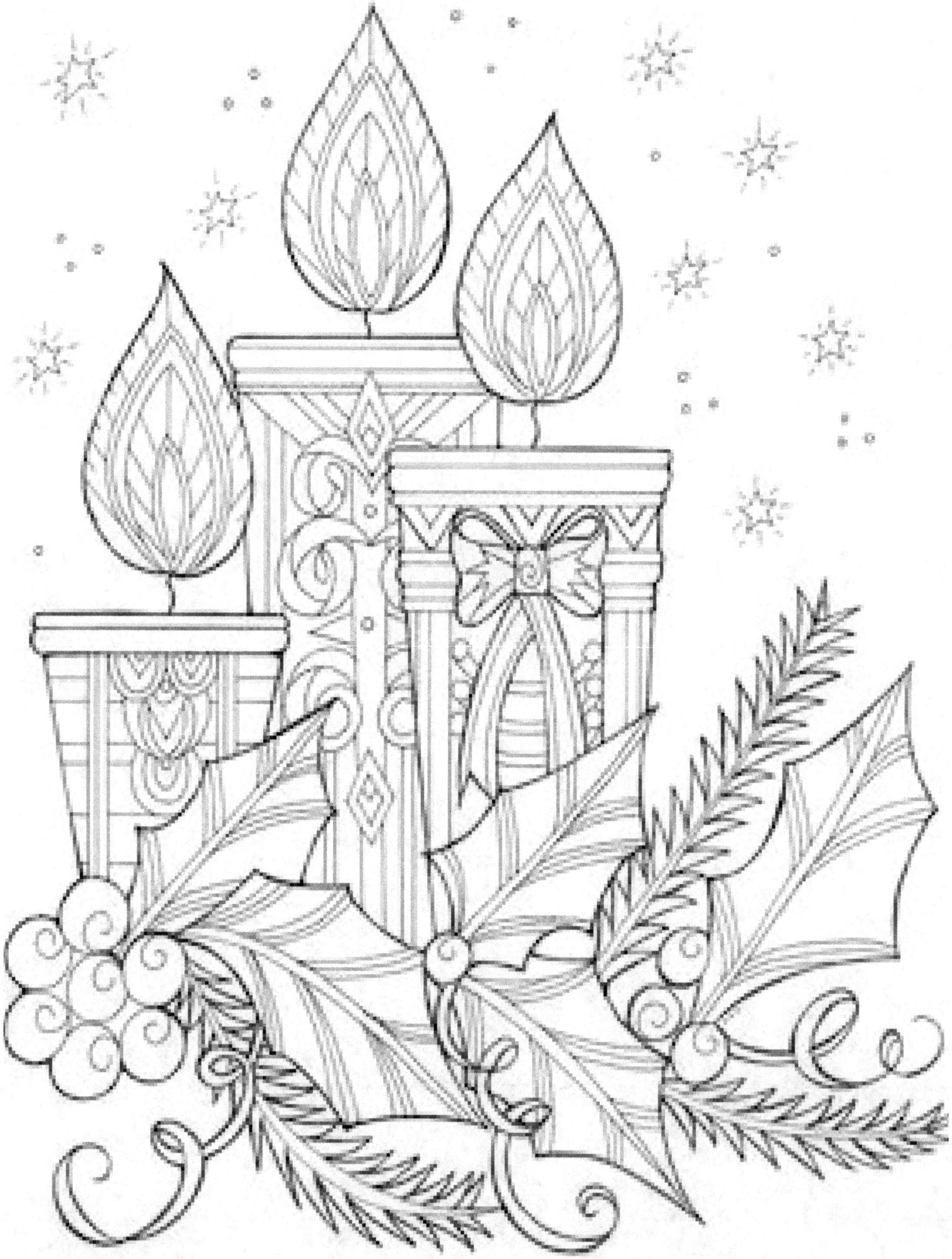

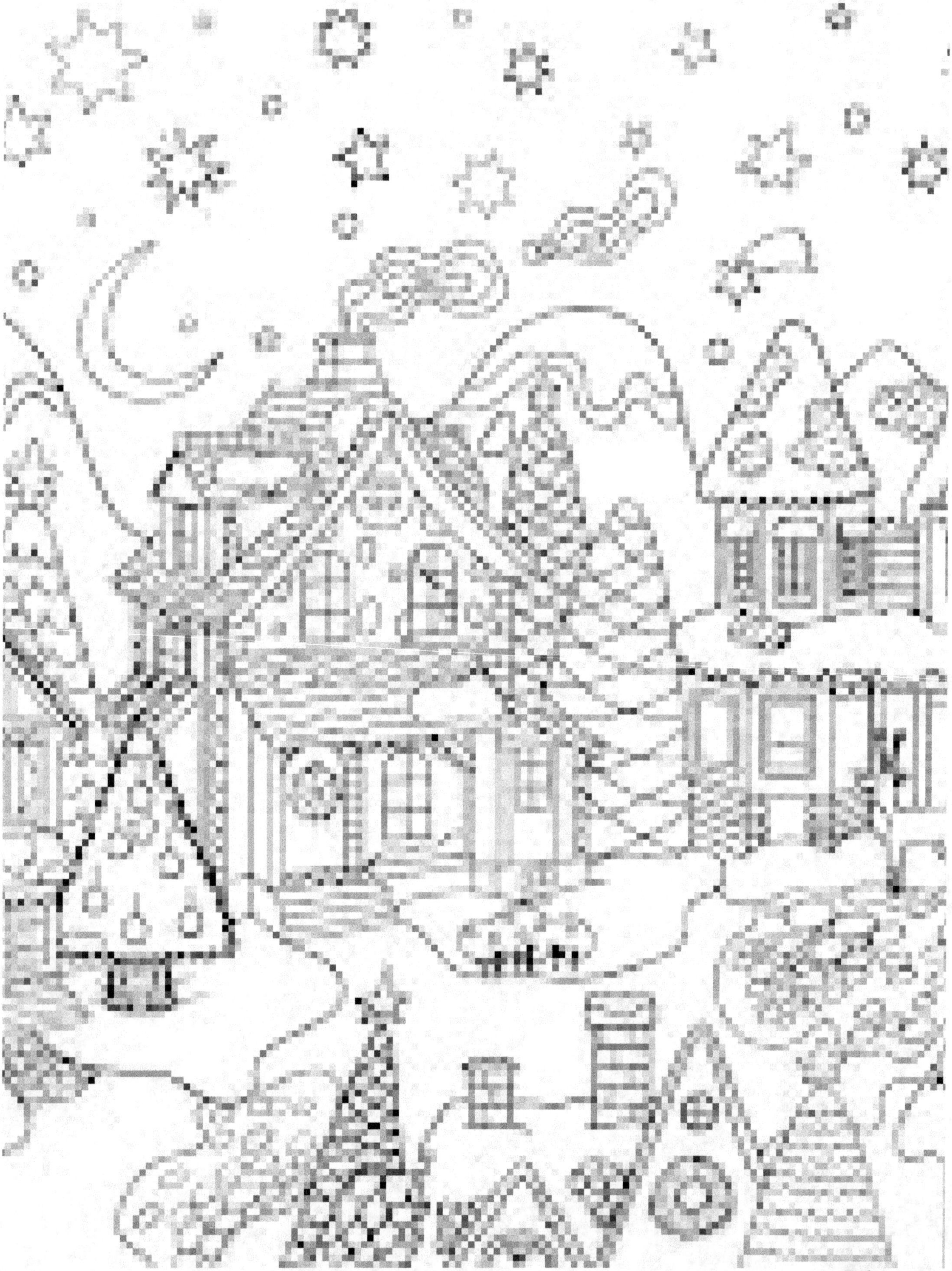

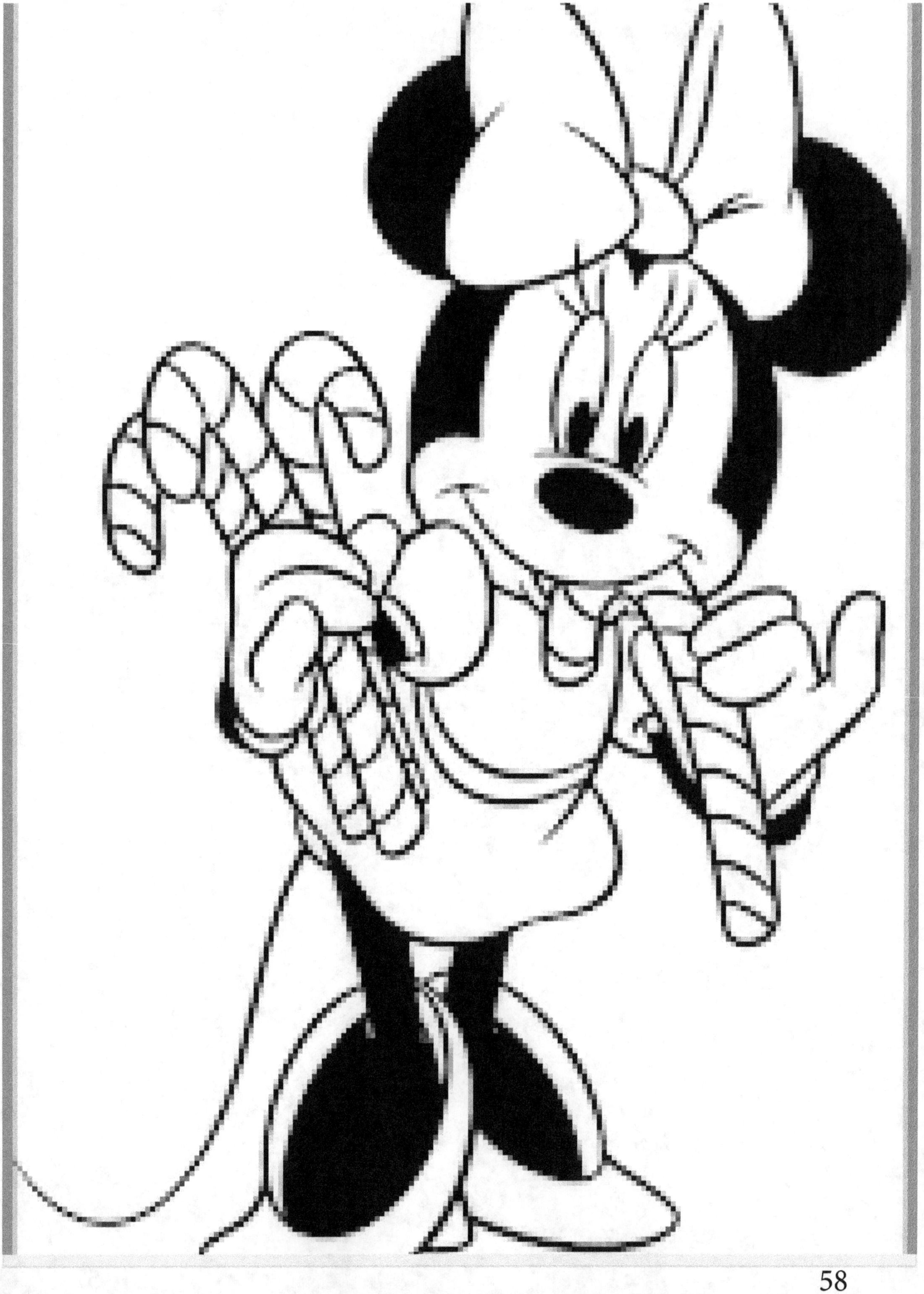

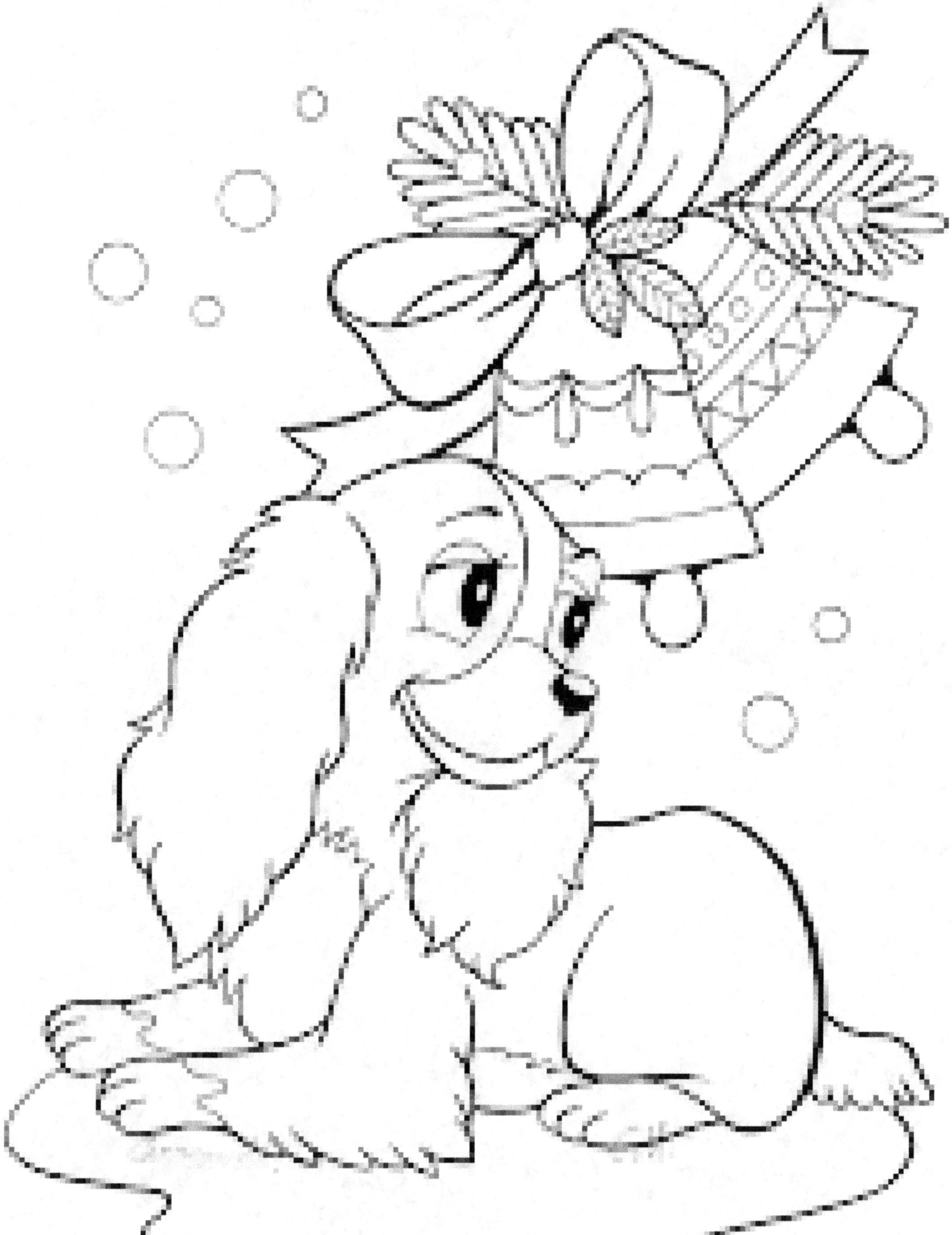

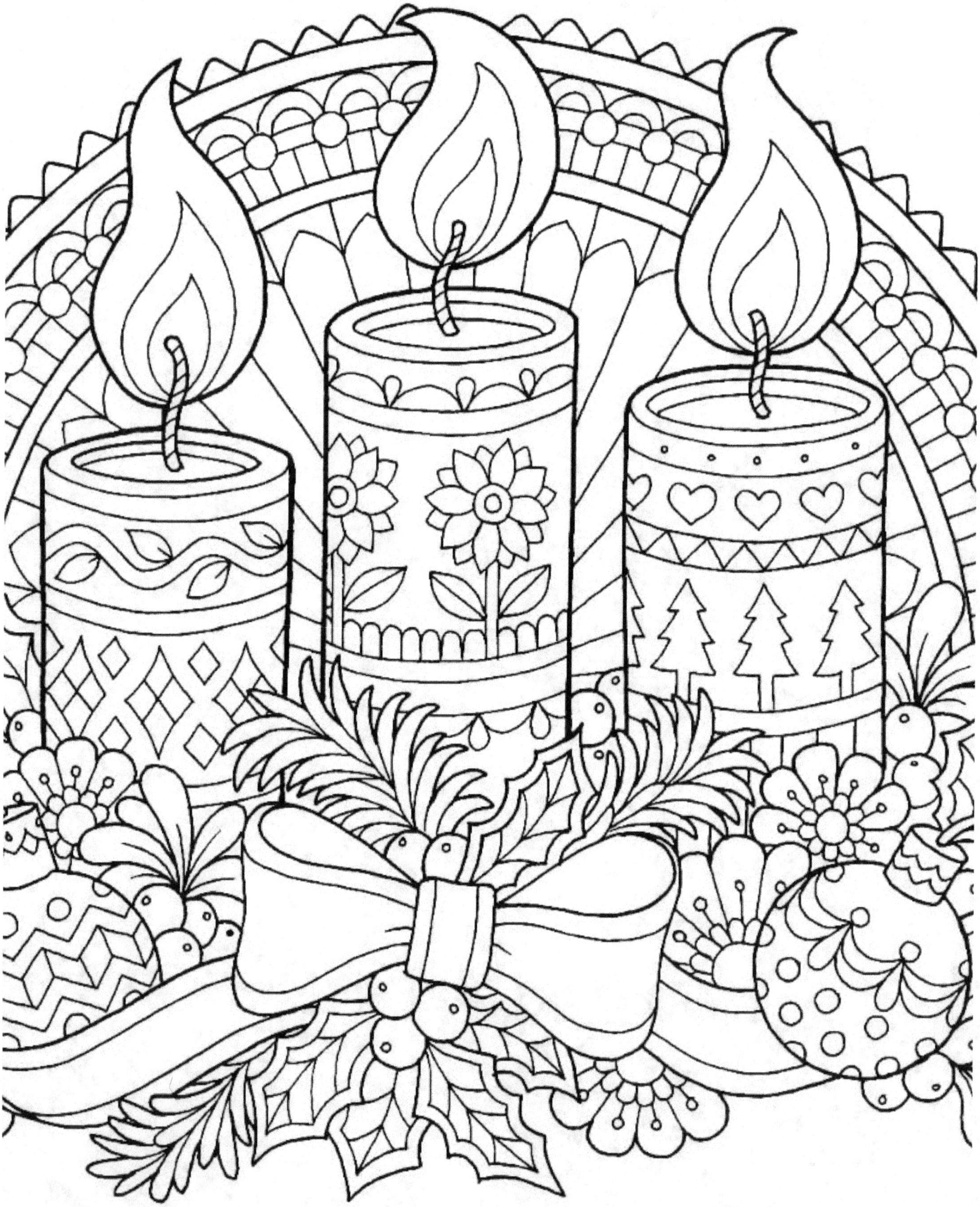

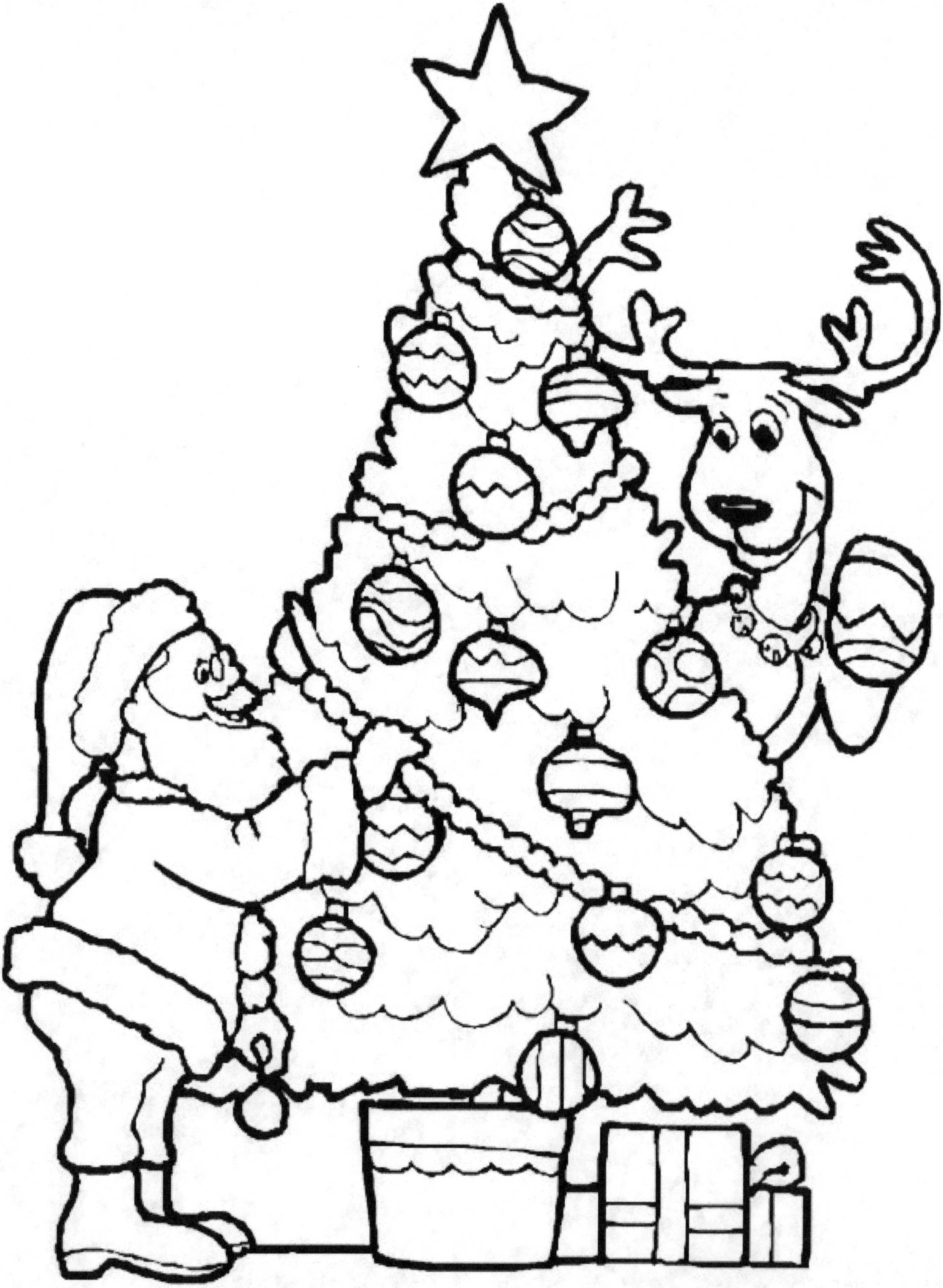

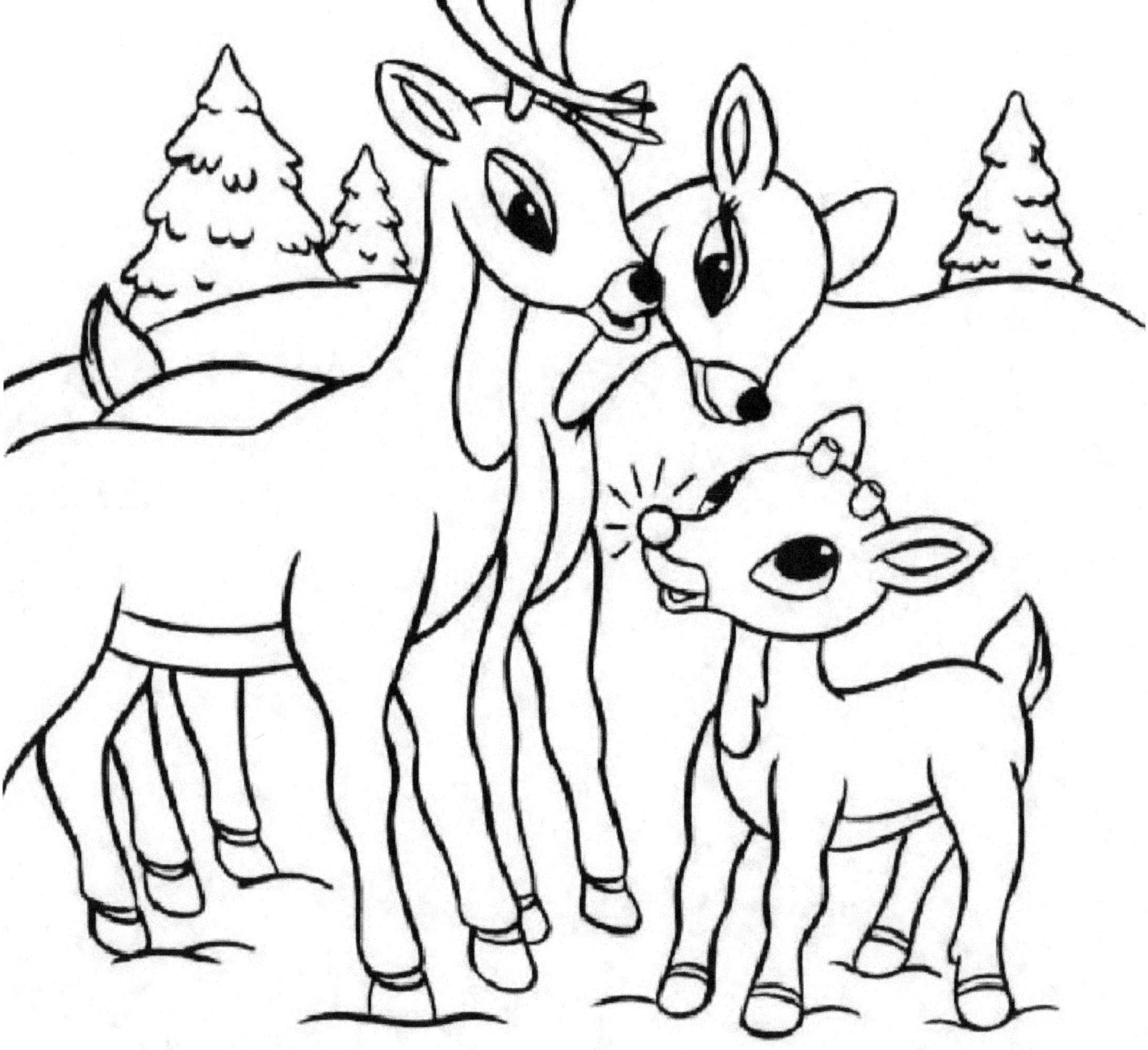

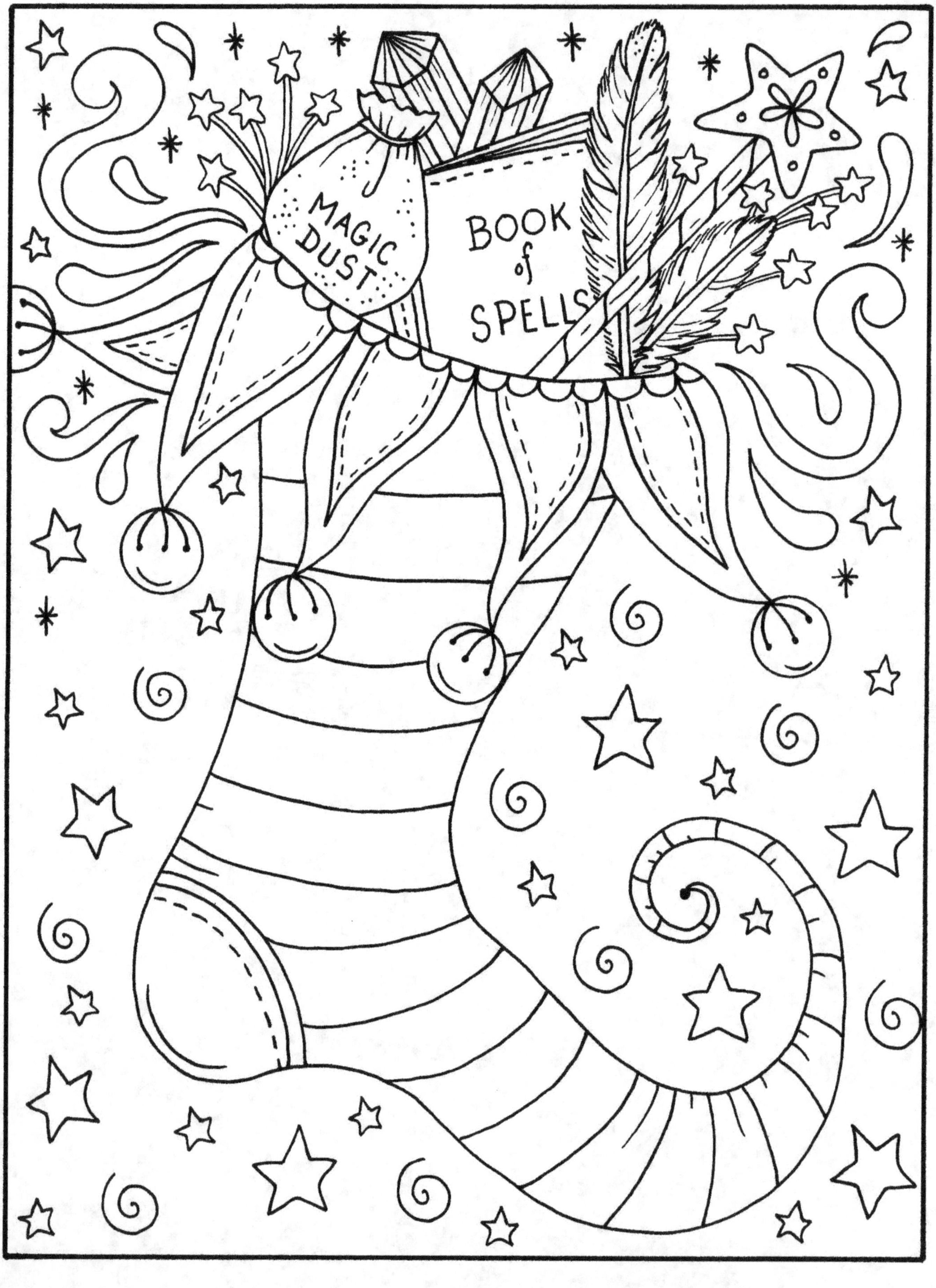
MAGIC DUST
BOOK of SPELLS

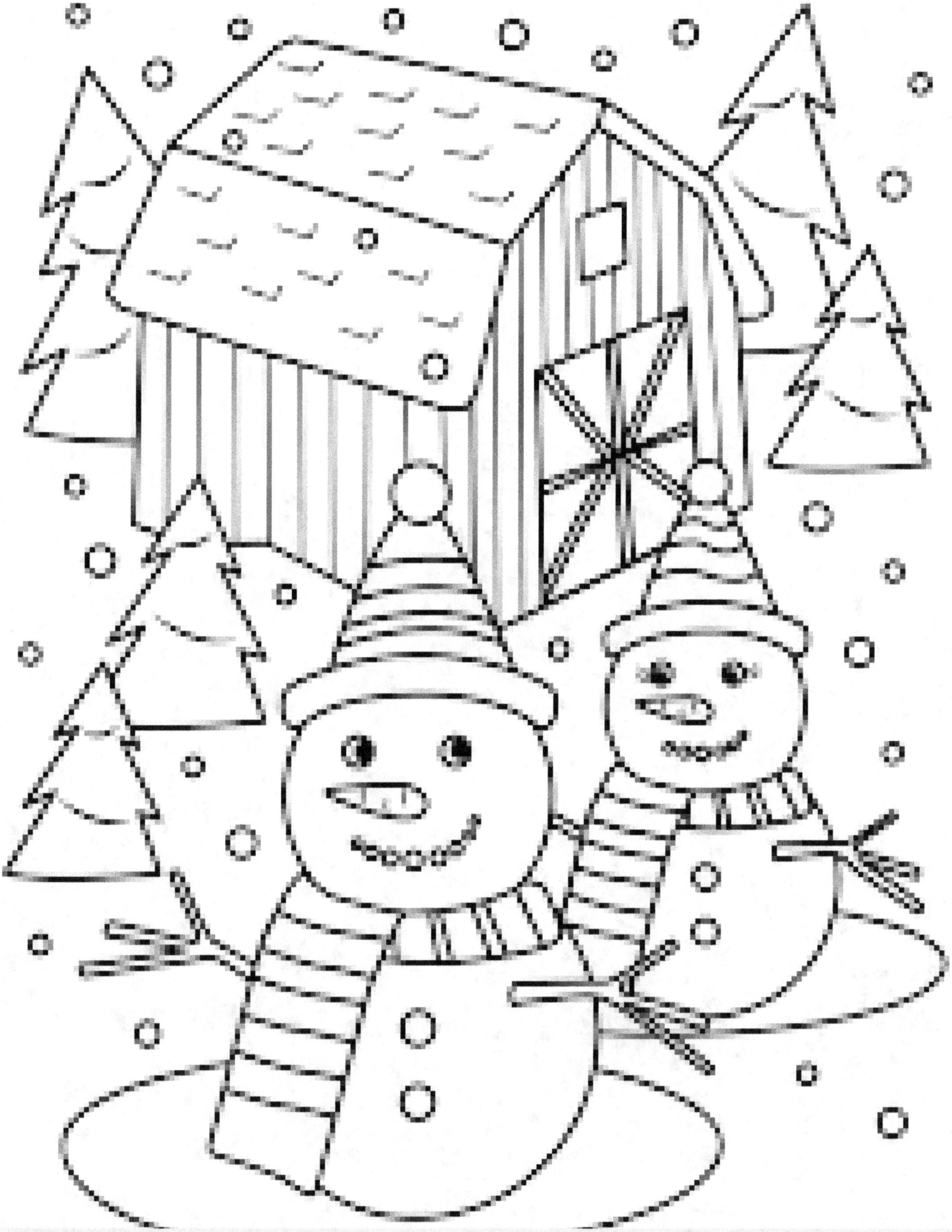

www.ingramcontent.com/pod-product-compliance
Lightning Source LLC
Chambersburg PA
CBHW080857220526
45467CB00008B/2532